MW01123900

FOOD TALK

FOOD TALK

A Man's Guide to Cooking
and Conversation with Women

H.L. (Bud) Goodall

A SNOWGOOSE COVE BOOK

6 Snowgoose Cove, Greensboro, North Carolina 27455

Published by Snowgoose Cove Publishing
6 Snowgoose Cove
Greensboro, NC 27455

Copyright © 1998 by Snowgoose Cove Publishing

Text copyright © 1998 by H. L. Goodall

All rights reserved. No part of this book may be reproduced or transmitted in any form or by any means,
electronic or mechanical, including photocopying, recording, or by any information storage and retrieval
system, without the written permission of the Publisher, except where permitted by law.

Food Talk by H. L. (Bud) Goodall
Library of Congress Catalog Number: 98-9033
Goodall, H. Lloyd

Food Talk / H. Lloyd Goodall

p. cm.
ISBN 0-9664053-0-7
1. Cooking   2. Communication and Culture – United States

Printed in the United States of America
June 1998
10 9 8 7 6 5 4 3 2 1

Cheers!

Contents

THE RECIPES

Contents

Contents

Preface

Food Talk: A Man's Guide to Cooking and Conversation with Women is about how a man can learn to give a woman two things she craves: a well-cooked meal and improved conversation.

The idea for the cookbook emerged one evening as I was preparing dinner for my wife, Sandra. It was a simple dish that took about twenty minutes to prepare—a wild mushroom pasta laced with warmed pecans, sautéed sun-dried tomatoes, and artichokes—one that always wins big smiles at our table. One of our neighbors walked into the kitchen with Sandra and openly marveled at my work. She said something like "Gosh, I wish my husband cooked like that!" This is a line that I have heard repeated by many women, many times, over the years. I thanked her for the compliment, smiled, and continued cooking.

"The fact is, your husband *can learn to* cook like this," replied Sandra. "All it takes is convincing Bud to make his next book a cookbook." The unspoken context for this assertion is the fact that I am by profession a teacher of, and a writer about, communication, as well as an accomplished cook.

"Would you?" Said our elated neighbor. "I mean, *really?*"

"Sure, I can see it now: *Dr. Bud's Cookbook for Men Who Like to Eat But Have Significant Others or Wives Who Don't Cook*," I said, joining in the fun.

My wife looked at our neighbor, and our neighbor looked at my wife.

"Not bad," they replied in unison.

Sandra edited the title to something like *Men Cooking for Women, For a Change*. She suggested that many men needed to improve their communication skills as well as their cooking skills, which gave rise to the sections of the book dedicated to improved communication, specifically improved dinner conversation. It was a short step from my basic classroom premise—that shared talk creates and constitutes the meaning of human realities—to the idea that the practice of romance had as much to do with talk as it does with learning how to cook. In this sense, "cooking" is really just a metaphor for a wide variety of romantic, *communicative* activities that two people can learn to share.

How to Use This Book

The idea behind this project is a simple one. Most men like to learn to do one thing at a time, and do it well. It doesn't matter if the aim is improved skill at a game, such as baseball or golf, or using a new computer software package, men learn methodically, and we are most happy when we can acquire and master one skill set at a time. For this reason men often say "just tell me what I need to know to get the job done." And, by and large, this is fine. We learn one skill set at a time, and work toward mastery of it.

However, most cookbooks are not written from a male user's perspective. They assume that if you can read, you can cook. For most men, it is not that easy. If it were, many of us would have learned to cook long ago. The problem is *not* that most men don't know how to read, or even want to read; it is *how and why we read* that makes all the difference.

Our reading logic is based on our propensity *to learn how to do one thing at a time*, and then adapt those procedures and that skill set to more complex applications. Male learning is also highly dependent upon conceptually linking that which we don't know much about—in this case, cooking—with something we do know something about—in this case, the management and coordination of a simple project.

In this way, learning to cook becomes a familiar process that requires organization, the acquisition of raw materials, the right tools, and the steps (or blueprint) required to complete the job. Men learn in order to *do*.

This book is written accordingly. I begin each chapter with a fool-proof recipe, reduce its perceived mysteries to simple steps and skills, and then provide ways in which what is learned from mastering this skill set can be expanded into other menu options. The result is a book that can not only teach anyone to cook, but one that instills the value of continuous learning in the kitchen.

Cooking Lessons are Communication Lessons

While meditating on the nature of recipes and how I could adapt them for men, I became aware of what it was that I really offer. My cooking lessons go beyond "just getting the job done" in the kitchen. At first I thought it was just a way to get men to think differently about food.

But it is really more than that. It is a way to translate how we can learn to think about preparing food for the one we love, or want to love, into opportunities for real *dialogue* with her. In this book, learning to cook is really learning how to improve your intimate *communication*. Just as cooking well improves the quality of your life, communicating well improves the quality of your relationships.

I accomplish this task in two ways.

First, I begin the book with a series of warm-up exercises designed to acquaint you with fundamentals of cooking and communicating with women. In these sections I translate current research and theory about gender and communication into language that men can understand and act on while discussing the basics of planning meals, organizing a kitchen, and overcoming supermarket dread.

Second, each chapter opens with a story about food that is also a metaphor about relationships. Then, at the end of each chapter I provide an intimate communication lesson. For example, in the sandwich chapter I begin with how to improve small talk. In the salads chapter I discuss the importance and skills of good relational listening. In the pasta chapter I explain what men communicate to women while we are dining. In subsequent chapters I provide advice on telling your life story and listening to her's, being more honest when communicating, engaging in romantic dialogue, developing a sense of humor, improving intimate eye contact and facial expressions, communicating appropriately "the morning after," understanding her need for relational definition, issues of power and control between women and men, and, finally, ways of honoring your relationship.

Communication is how we construct and live within our intimate relationships, just as cooking is the way we construct the essence of fine dining. This book, then, really is about giving women the *two* things they really want: A man who can prepare a delicious dinner *and* engage them in meaningful conversations.

Acknowledgments

No book about cooking or relationships is ever written without the assistance of many other people. This one owes special debts of thanks to many men and women who have contributed their culinary experiences, ideas, stories, and recipes, including my mother, Naomi Saylor Goodall; my grandmother, Nellie Grimm Saylor; Moe and Marian Auyash, who introduced me to the exotic delights in Greek and Spanish foods; Pete Kellett, my British friend, communication colleague, lunch master, and workout pal; Clarence and Martha Bray, my dear friends who happen to be my in-laws (with a special thanks to Clarence for doing yeoman service as a copyeditor for this book!); Kris, Bob, and Gene Bess, our Utahian Tex-Mex experts; Stew Auyash and Patti Zimmerman, our Ithaca friends who enjoy good food and meaningful talk as much as we do; Chris and Alice Waagen, who taught me how to cook well on a grad school budget; Nancy Phillips, who, with her husand Gerry, used one memorable Thanksgiving dinner to reveal the secrets of a writing life; Eric Eisenberg and Lori Roscoe, our Tampa food talk connection; Renee and Russell MacDonald, who rave about my leftovers; Christianna and Eric Anthony, whose charred pizza dinner helped inspire this volume; the Lake Jeanette "only light appetizers" and card-playing crowd; Elizabeth Taggart, who taught me the joys of Korean cooking (and who contributed recipes and techniques for California Rolls, Sesame Spinach, and Cucumber salad to this book) and her Bailey's cake-baking husband Chris; Drew Thompson, ace guitarist, sound man, and steak chef; the other members of the "Crazy Eights": Barry Bell and Lori Lindbergh, Jody Natalle and Larry Hyjek, Ansley Brown and Joyce Ferguson, who eat and talk better than anybody has a right to; Carl and Susan Lovitt, our Clemson pals who always have a good excuse for organizing conversations around good food; Rosa Collins, the reigning queen of Chattanooga cuisine; Rick and Jackie Bray, Kate Bray and Richard Heston, who bring four distinct traditions to family get-togethers.

No cookbook author is ever without culinary heroes and heroines, either. Large on my list of inspiring culinary artists and writers: James Beard, Julia Child, Betty Crocker, Paul Prudhomme, Mark Miller, Martha Stewart, Craig Claiborne, Jim Harrison, Sheila Lukins, and Julee Rosso. And no writer about human communication is without influences. Mine include Plato, Aristotle, Quintilian, and Cicero; George Campbell and Bishop Whately; Kenneth Burke, Mikhail Bakhtin, George Herbert Mead, and Herbert Blumer; Ellen Bersheid and Elaine Walster, Gerald M. Phillips, Edna Rodgers, William Rawlins, Barbara Montgomery, Leslie Baxter, Steve Duck, Rod Hart, Don Burks, Bob Carlson, and Julia T. Wood.

This book truly could not have become what it is without the hard work and strong support of the Snowgoose Cove Publishing team. This is a publishing company that values the acquisitions and managing editors, publicity and marketing directors, artist and author as equal stakeholders. Together, we create a vision for a book; research, write, and develop it; then organize a coordinated campaign to get it into the hands of people who can benefit from it. For this reason, I owe a deep and very special debt of gratitude to Sandra Goodall, Paula Pilson, Diana Dalton, Jon McLean, and Nic Goodall.

But most of all *Food Talk* is indebted to the abiding influence and love of good food and good conversation shared with my wife, Sandra. It is for her, and because of her, that this book truly *cooks*.

WARM UP EXERCISES

"Communication is a craft ... like cookery."

—*Plato,* The Gorgias

WHAT DO WOMEN WANT?

In America, when men learn how to cook well for women

they acquire a special identity. This identity enhances their

personal relationships as well as deepens their enjoyment

of food. Looked at this way, a man who has learned how

to cook has another way to create meaning through

shared experiences. This is because in addition to our

bodies' need for basic nutrition, what women *and* men

are truly hungry for are meaningful experiences and

genuine communication that shape a well-lived life.

Cooking and Communication

Men who learn to cook well often do well with women. In part this is because eating good food together is a shared sensual experience that nourishes the body, reduces stress, alleviates boredom, enhances conversation, speaks to the spirit, and enlivens the heart. And in part it is because women don't expect it. It is a rare man who can walk confidently into a kitchen and do something more than open a can or throw together a bland sandwich. It is a rare man who appreciates the finer things in life, who takes time for sensual pleasures, who understands and knows how to be creative with food, and who takes pride in being able to make every day a little more romantic, and special.

> Bottom line: learning to cook well is an important way to demonstrate that you know how to give a woman what she really wants. It is a path to better and more intimate communication. And, as a major side benefit, you eat well too.

Bucking Tradition

Why is it, then, that most men don't know how to cook? The answer is not in some mysterious missing gene that prevents us from learning our way around a kitchen. The truth is that the reason most men claim not to be able to cook is purely sociological.

Historically and socially there has been a strict separation of home and work that defined a kind of basic partnership for living a life together. Men worked outside the home; women worked in the home, which included responsibility for preparing meals. However, the rules have changed. Women in large numbers have entered the work force outside the home and men, in growing numbers, are seeking more time at home with their families. Women have learned how to change the oil in a car, manage the family's finances, and become more assertive in the office; men have learned how to clean apartments and houses, spend quality time with children, and organize the family's meals.

Despite these changes, most men still don't cook. Many of us would rather pick up the phone and order a greasy pizza, or drive to the local plastic palace of overpriced and heart-menacing burgers, or try to get by on dry cereal, rather than open a cookbook and prepare a decent, tasty, and economical meal. Why?

The answer is simple. Many men are still trapped in an illogical, old-fashioned, and largely irrelevant image of manhood. Regularly, we humble ourselves by attempting to pump more iron at the gym than our bodies can handle, obsess about the stats of our favorite dead sports heroes, or even spend big money to chase tiny white balls around a green field with a long stick; but *cooking*? Well, never! We would rather go into long-term marriage counseling than learn to cook. In my experience, there are four basic reasons for this:

1. Many men still associate cooking with "women's work," despite the fact that we all love to eat and most of what we love to eat isn't eaten raw.

2. We associate preparing a meal with the ineffable mysteries of womanhood, despite the fact that any man who can put a video in a VCR, or use a computer to surf the net, can follow basic instructions to create a meal.

3. Many men feel that if they don't already know how to do something, they should—on principle—simply refuse to learn. This is at least as ridiculous as our well-documented fear of risking manhood by asking directions. Taken in tandem—refusing to learn something new and refusing to admit we don't know where we are—these refusals go a long way toward defining us as precisely what most feminists claim us to be: hopeless Neanderthals.

4. We feel that if we demonstrate that we do have creative abilities in the kitchen, we will be called upon—or expected—to perform them regularly.

This last fear may, in fact, be well-founded. But the upside may well be that we eat a lot better and learn to enjoy the fine art of cooking well. Who knows, we may even be able to trade off on our new skill for something "manly" that we secretly don't like to do, such as mowing the lawn.

Guys: Admit it. The real reason you don't want to learn how to cook is not the act itself, but the *idea* of it. Like the big bad shark in the classic movie *Jaws*, the idea of it is what really threatens the very essence of who you are, who you claim to be. Not just who you are for yourself. But for *her*. For *them*. None of the aforementioned fears, nor even the force of all of them conspiring together, really make a damn bit of difference. The shark in *Jaws* was a man-made eating machine created out of a long-standing myth; your fears about cooking are a collection of powerful but stupid ideas about what it means to be "a man."

Come on, *face it*. The first step in Dr. Bud's 12-Step Plan for Cooking Recovery is facing the fact that your fear of cooking is really just a symptom of a deeper mythic fear about who you are. As a man. As a manly man. And about what a manly man can't—or shouldn't—learn how to do.

Pretty ridiculous, huh? You know I'm right. Go on, *admit* it.

Now, let me help you.

Reinventing Our Image

Just as we decided what manhood was in days past, we can decide to reinvent manhood today. We can consider the preparation of food a natural part of a more fully evolved articulation of manliness. It can become a part of the total statement you make about who you are, what you know, and what you can do *as a man*.

You, too, can become a man who, in addition to everything else he does well, *cooks*. A man who has *no fears anywhere*, certainly none that might occur in such a dangerous and foreboding place as the kitchen in your own apartment or home.

I mean what are you afraid of? Toasters, for God's sake? Big bad ovens? Those nasty old pots and pans? How to use knives, forks, and spoons? Recipe books with steps that a six year-old can follow? The evil that may invade your life if you give up dining out of a can or bid farewell to the old college standby, Top Ramen noodles?

Get a grip, fella. There is a lot more to fear underneath the hood of your car (a series of gasoline-induced controlled explosions, for example) or driving to work (need I say lane-swerving lunatics screaming into cell phones) than in the average kitchen. *Your* kitchen. Your kitchen in *your* home. And hey, aren't we supposed to be the masters of our own homes?

Look at it this way: *many of the world's great chefs are men*. This is no accident. For centuries truly inspired men have cooked well. Many have used their culinary expertise to add a creative dimension to their total experience of life, to their work as well as their relationships, to their lovemaking as well as their caregiving. To *not* rise to the culinary challenge is to risk being more than just a little disappointing to the one you're with; it is to render yourself, as a man, not only relatively unevolved, but—sigh—clearly and entirely *ordinary*. Is this what you want?

No way. No *real* man would.

Real men lead. Any time, anywhere, certainly any place.

Real men accept challenges, approach what lesser men take-for-granted with a repertoire of new questions and available possibilities.

Real men work well with new ideas, with weights and measurements, with tools, with precise formulas and calculations.

Real men find the poetic in the use of otherwise everday things.

Real men learn from differences, as well as contribute to them. Most importantly, real men are always willing to acquire new understandings and skills, both to perfect their technique as well as to transform them.

All of this is to say that real men can learn to do some of their best work in the kitchen. Let us begin.

GETTING A GAME PLAN

Planning a meal is a lot like preparing a presentation for

a meeting. You need to establish a goal and then

create an interesting and memorable message

designed to help you reach that goal. You need to

organize and present your message with skill and style.

Think of cooking this way, and you will learn to

approach meal planning as efficiently and skillfully as

any other task.

Let's examine this basic game plan for meal planning in greater detail. First, you need to establish a goal for the dinner. The trick here is to rely on what the ancient Romans called *imagio*, the ability to use your imagination to come up with an organizing idea. The key is to develop answers for the following questions:

What mood do you want to inspire? What category of main dish— pasta, chicken, red meat, pork, seafood—do you naturally associate with that mood?

For example, is what you are after a lighthearted get-together or a serious romantic discussion? Are you planning to use this dinner as a place to launch your plan to see whether this relationship is ready to move to another level, or are you content with the way things are? Are you both in the mood for something sinful, or for something deeper, perhaps even more soulful? For details on what each category of food rhetorically suggests, see the opening section for each chapter in this book.

What category of food does she enjoy?

The art of persuasion begins with the assumption that every form of talk must be adapted to the needs and expectations of its listeners. In this way, you need to prepare food that *she* likes to eat, but not necessarily that she has had before. If you know she is a vegetarian, don't fix steak and expect a positive reaction. If you aren't sure what she likes to eat, go with chicken. Chicken is usually a safe bet. Just in case, have a salad and a vegetable.

Work within the basic categories, but expand the known boundaries creatively. For details on how to accomplish this, read the basic recipe that begins each chapter, then study the alternatives.

How can you ensure you create the mood you are striving for?

Think of a dinner as an setting that induces certain kinds of talk and reduces the possibility of others. What you want to do is plan a meal in relation to your desire for a memorable evening. Memorable evenings are created out of exchanges of memorable messages, of talk that matters, of enriching and deepening your understanding and appreciation of each other. Because food and talk are both primary sources of sustenance, they should work together. What message is being suggested by your choice of main dish? By your appetizers? By the side dishes? The dessert?

Third, *what type of stylistic embellishments can you add to the presentation or enhance the mood?*

Would a single red rose in a glass vase centered on the table help? Or would it be too much? Can a few sprigs of parsley over the potatoes make the appearance of the dinner more attractive? Are there condiments that ought to be served with the dishes you preparing? If so, do you have appropriate serving dishes for them? Does this dinner demand cloth napkins? Soft music? To answer these questions, consider your presentation from her point of view.

Women connect everything to everything else. She will perceive intention and purpose *regardless* of whether or not you do. Plan accordingly.

Fourth, *what "talking points" do you hope to pursue during dinner?*

What questions can you ask? What statements ought you make? How can what you plan to talk about be organized—should one topic naturally occur before another? How will you know if you have been successful? What can you do if you aren't successful?

Speak from your heart. *Always.*

The Challenge of Communicating with Women

One of the major differences between women and men is that we have very distinctive communication styles. According to many scholars and relational therapists, men's style can be summed up as giving "reports" intended to influence outcomes or opinions. Women, on the other hand, communicate to build "rapport." Because we come at talk in different ways and for different outcomes, all too often we find ourselves wondering why we attempted to communicate in the first place. However, once you understand the basis for these differences, your communication with women can improve.

Women Talk To Build Relationships, Men Talk to Control

Women tend to view talk as the "substance" of their relationships. They show this by using statements like "I know *just* how you feel," or "that happened to me, just last week. " Rarely will you hear men say these things.

Why not? Because men use talk as a way of obtaining goals or influencing ends. Our speech is typically about exerting influence or control, building up our status, or stressing how independent and "manly" we are. We may, in fact, have "been there," and "done that," but unless we can use that fact as evidence of how cool or sophisticated we are, we generally leave it alone. This is especially true if the "been there, done that" refers to something that makes us appear foolish, or proves that we have been "bested" by another person.

By contrast, women often *connect* with each other through admissions of mistakes, errors in judgment, or general foolishness. Men, unless drunk, tend to avoid these sources of identification because we think they make us sound weak.

Women Talk About Everything, Men Report

Women build relationships and closeness by talking a lot, about everything. Communication scholars refer to this as "processing information," or "doing maintenance work," and the basic rule is that women are *always* "processing," always doing relational maintenance work. What men don't realize is that, "Honey, how was your day?" is a *real* question for women. Women ask these questions to gain information about your experiences, and to show that they care about us.

Men, by contrast, don't generally feel a need to do as much processing because our job, as men, is simply *to report* on the world we live in. "How was your day?" is perceived by men as a relatively meaningless question, on par with the "hi, how are you?" kind of small talk at work that requires only a cursory response. Our typical answer to these types of questions tend to be a simple, and short, naming of events followed by either the click of the TV coming on or the rustle of the paper being raised. And we wonder why we get the cold shoulder for the rest of the evening. To add insult to injury, we seldom ask the same question of her, which makes us appear as if we don't care what kind of day she has had. See the difference, and the challenge here?

Women Care About Outcomes, Men Assert

Women tend to be more tentative in their assertions or conclusions, whereas most men boldly assert whatever is on our minds. Have you ever noticed how some women tend to "tag" the ends of what should be sentences with question marks? Why is this? Because women are always working with alternative explanations to find sources of support that allow them to seem as if they are remaining open, and therefore building rapport, in order to maintain relationships.

> Men, by contrast, are usually more interested in being right, or getting others to agree with us, of getting to the point, often even at the expense of otherwise close and important relationships. We don't require as much feedback to what we say because, well, what would be the point? The point is that when we don't ask her opinion or solicit feedback to our ideas, we are showing ourselves to be self-centered, close-minded, and generally unsupportive.

So what can we do to improve our communication style with women? Think of a conversation like a really good tennis match. The best matches allow for a long series of volleys. Each person is so into the game that together, they become engrossed. Questions allow you to volley, keeping the conversation in play. Statements end the conversation. You might win the point, but you will never win the match. Watch these patterns in your own relationships and analyze the results. If your desire for creating a better relationship is important to you, and if you find that stubbornly sticking to a masculine style is getting in the way of a good relationshp, maybe there is a little room for change.

Dinner Talk, Changing the Pattern

Do you know what the Number One complaint women have about men during dinner dates?

We talk too much about ourselves.

I want you to think about that fact in relation to your own behavior. Does it ring true? Come on, be honest about it. This is just you and me here.

If so, don't panic. This is not necessarily a sign of your deep narcissism. Or conceit. Or rampant ego. It does not necessarily mean that you could care less about her, or that the only thing that really matters *to* you *is* you.

Those things are definitely true of some guys, *other* guys. But *not* you. Not a stand-up, caring, sensitive, evolved fellow such as yourself. Right?

Right.

So this is what you need to do to overcome that small problem.

> First, take a clue from the Big Lesson taught for years by none other than Dale Carnegie: To influence people to like you and to want to be with you, what you need to do is to get them to talk about themselves.

Translation for the mentally challenged: Ask *her* to talk about *her*self.

Chances are very good that she will want to. Women believe in the rapport-building virtues of shared personal talk. Probably she will talk about her life, her job, her family, her interests. Just like you do, when you talk about yourself. Except that you are going to do less of that, remember?

But it is okay if she does it. In fact, you want to encourage her to.

Don't complain that this isn't fair because she gets to do it and you don't. Life isn't always about what's fair, and in matters of talk between women and men, this is just the way it is. Deal with it.

> Now, the less evolved version of the contemporary male will read this page, decide to follow my advice and actually ask her to talk about herself, but then won't really listen. You know what I mean. He'll *act* like he's listening, but his thoughts will be mind-surfing elsewhere. He may be thinking about the food, then about something that is bothering him at work, then about a moment in his childhood, then he may wonder—in typical *When Harry Met Sally* fashion—how good she will be in bed, and what his chances of getting her there are, etc.

But this is a big mistake. Most women can tell whether or not you are listening to them. And whether you are listening to them or not matters a great deal to them. They have even devised devilish little tests to see how well or closely we have been listening, such as the asking for our opinion of what they have just uttered, or inquiring as to whether or not we would like to do that. Huh? Do What?

If your answer sounds like that, you might as well call it an evening. You've blown it. Big time.

And, not because you *are* an ape, but because you haven't ever practiced the fine art of listening. For the more fully evolved among us, the advice to ask her to talk about herself will be closely coupled with the idea that you should, in fact, listen to what she says. Listen *carefully*. Listen with empathy. Listen with an open mind. All of those good things.

But also listen for *patterns*. Gregory Bateson, an eminent anthropologist, taught us that communication is pattern recognition. This means you should listen for clues that connect the dots in the story she is telling about herself. These clues can be core attitudes, values, or beliefs that inform a wide range of topics. Or they can be an overall emotional tone that provides evidence of how she feels about this or that. Or they can be events that stand as symbolic moments in her life, moments that determined or defined aspects of her understanding, her experience, her character.

The more fully evolved man listens for patterns for two reasons:

The first reason is because it provides informational opportunities to engage her in meaningful conversation. By cueing in on what she is saying and comparing it to what you think, feel, or have experienced, you can figure out where you agree and disagree. Both are good entry points for any conversation. The talk will usually move rather quickly from a monologue to a dialogue, with a healthy dose of give-and-take leading not only to shared understandings and feelings, but perhaps to the kind of real communication that both of you long for. This is a very good thing.

The second reason you want to listen is because some patterns are disturbing. Unless you are paying attention, you won't hear those sources of information that should cause large alarms to go off in your head and heart. We've all had experiences with certain types of women that we ought not repeat. Unfortunately, many men repeat the same mistakes with the same types of women because they just weren't listening. This is a very bad thing.

Okay, now that we've established that you should get her to talk about herself and that you should pay close attention to what she says, what else can you do to develop talk during dinner? I recommend developing a short list of "talking points"—interesting things to talk about with her—*prior* to your date. Spend a few minutes jotting down or memorizing key issues of interest to both of you, and figure out how and perhaps when you might bring them up.

Is she interested in movies? Great. Now, what type of movies? Did she see the newest film in that genre? What did she think about the way the director handled a particular scene? How about literature? What does she like to read? Same thing. International politics? NASCAR? Whatever.

Get the idea? Remember, the successful communicator adapts his talk to her interests, her needs, and what she thinks about. From there, you can develop a dialogue. But first, you need to show good faith.

See how that works? With a little preparation, you too will be able to go into the dinner talk arena with greater confidence because you have a *communication plan*.

TOOLING UP

Does your kitchen resemble something out of a horror

movie? Do smells emanate from your refrigerator in

ways that attract the serious and sustained attention of

the neighbors' dogs? Was your pantry last cleaned

when your mother visited? If the answer to any or all of

these questions is affirmative, then perhaps you need to

spend a little time cleaning and organizing your kitchen

for the same level of efficiency and productivity

undoubtedly found in your office.

Basic Kitchen Knowledge

Think of your kitchen as an extension of your office. Now walk into it. What do you see?

Is it clean, well lit, and well organized? Are your cabinets and their contents neatly arranged? Does your refrigerator reflect a sense of order? Have you assembled all the tools necessary to do the job? Is your answer "yes"? Excellent! You are ready to begin.

Or is your answer "no"? Tell the truth.

Creating a clean, well-lit, and well-organized kitchen is an essential part of becoming a good cook. No matter how large or small your workspace, the important ideas are:

1. Your kitchen should feel good when you step into it. It must be clean, well-lit, sensibly arranged, and alive with creative possibilities. Living things—such as plants, humans, and pets—should flourish here. This will enhance your experience of cooking as well as channel the appropriate "chi"—or life energy—into the preparation of the food.

2. Appliances must be in good working order. Broken toasters and old food processors should be recycled. Get rid of everything that doesn't complement the activities associated with food preparation.

3. Do not use the kitchen as a storehouse for anything except food and the instruments of its preparation. Get rid of those stacks and piles of once-meaningful or meaningless stuff (newspapers, junk mail, magazines, etc.) that currently decorate what once was designed to be a countertop.

4. Organize your shelves and cabinets for maximum efficiency. For example:

   ■ Pots, pans, and skillets should be neatly arranged near the stove or range; plates, glassware, cups, and silverware should be located between the sink and dishwasher.

   ■ Reserve at least one drawer for measuring spoons and specialized cooking instruments (such as meat thermometers or veggie peelers).

   ■ Collect all devices designed to open things (manual can openers, corkscrews, and etc.) in another drawer, close to the trash and recycling bins.

5. Get rid of anything that is broken, rusted, won't ever work, or doesn't match your current dinnerware, glassware, or silverware. Chances are good that you will never make the time to repair or restore them, and besides, they take up space that can be used for other, more productive, purposes. One word of caution: If you are in a relationship, check with your significant other before tossing out anything. That tarnished platter that keeps falling on your head when you open the spice cabinet just might be a priceless heirloom!

6. Make sure that your countertops, sink(s), and other kitchen work areas (such as a butcher block) are clean and free of debris at all times. I recommend an anti-bacterial cleanser to be used on all surfaces after *each* meal preparation. Make sure your sink(s) is especially clean. Your floor should be spotless. Nothing promotes confidence in your abilities in the kitchen with others quite so much as a clean workspace. Would you eat something prepared in your kitchen? Then, why should she?

7. Your refrigerator also should be a clean, well-lit, and well-organized space. Remove all jars, bottles, cans, etc. and all foodstuffs and reorganize according to whatever systematic schema works best for you. I recommend organizing ingredients by height of the item, then by its purpose. For example:

- All condiments in my kitchen are stored on the refrigerator shelf doors, with large containers (ketchup, Worcestershire sauce, Soy sauce, etc.) on the bottom row, and smaller items (olives, pickles, small jars of mustards, etc.) higher.

- Reserve the most easily reachable space—such as the chest-level shelf on the door of the refrigerator—for large items you regularly use and return, such as milk, bottled water, and juice. Reserve one interior shelf for wine, soft drinks, and beer.

- Use one of the lower interior drawers for fresh fruits, ONLY; use another for fresh vegetables, ONLY; if your unit is equipped with a meats and/or cheeses drawer, use it for the purpose it was designed for.

- Do not keep a lot of stuff in your fridge that you won't use and nothing in it that is rotten or going bad.

- Invest in a box of baking soda, open it, and place it in the middle of the rear of your unit to neutralize odors; replace it once a month.

8. Your pantry should be arranged for easy identification and retrieval of canned, bagged, bottled, or boxed items. Think of it as a large filing cabinet. I recommend placing:

   ■ All cereals and crackers in one area; canned food in another; canned fruits in yet another.

   ■ Rice and pasta deserve their own place. Dried foodstuffs (such as peppers and mushrooms) do also.

   ■ Make nice straight lines with the cans, bottles, bags, and boxes.

   ■ Once again, get rid of anything that has past its expiration date, is unlikely to ever be used, or simply smells bad.

9. Onions and potatoes are perishable items and need to be kept in cool, dark, places. I recommend purchasing one of those netted bags for this purpose. Hang it in you pantry, if possible. If you do so, invest in a box of baking soda to cut the aroma. Check the bag once a week for any spoilage.

10. Place a wooden or ceramic bowl on your countertop and keep some fresh tomatoes or fruit in it. This will remind you to eat your vegetables and fruits, and it looks good in a kitchen.

11. Invest in a few green plants to decorate your kitchen area. Make sure you match the lighting and water needs of the plant with your particular kitchen location.

12. Reserve one major cabinet space for the organization of spices and seasonings. Arrange them alphabetically. Here are ones you will need; I've italicized the absolute basic necessities:

Basil

Bay leaves

Black Java pepper (coarse ground)

Cayenne pepper

Chili powder

Cloves (whole)

Coriander (Ground)

Cumin (Ground)

Curry powder

Dill weed

Garlic (preferably use fresh, but in a pinch, use powdered or minced)

Ginger (ground, fresh if possible)

Green peppercorns

Lemon pepper

Mustard (Ground)

Oregano

Paprika (mild or hot, you choose)

Parsley (fresh is best; dried is okay)

Red pepper flakes

Tarragon

Thyme

Vanilla extract

White pepper

Most dried spices kept in airtight containers can be stored for a long, long time. However, they do lose potency, and, therefore, purpose and utility. For this reason, I strongly recommend buying smaller amounts, using them regularly, and replenishing them often.

13. Display olive oils and flavored or aged vinegars on a countertop. Here is my list of what everyone who cooks should have on hand; again, the absolute necessities are italicized:

Extra virgin olive oil

Peanut oil

Red pepper oil

Sesame oil

Vegetable oil (canola, corn, or blended)

Balsamic vinegar (aged is best)

Raspberry vinegar

Red wine vinegar

Rice vinegar

White wine vinegar

14. Finally, my wife taught me a little secret that I'll share with you. Tile the wall behind your stove or range. This serves two goals: it enhances the look of your kitchen, and it protects your walls from grease splatters. Ceramic tiles are wonderful, but expensive. A less expensive option is to order contact paper (from William Sonoma, a catalog for cooks) that looks like ceramic tile and can be wiped clean with a sponge.

Now what do you think of your kitchen? See some things that need to be done? If you are living with someone, suggest making some of these improvements together. A word of caution, don't wave this book in your true love's face and chide her about the way the kitchen looks. You both live there right? You both eat? *You* could clean up the pantry all on your own and surprise her. Who knows where a little effort in the kitchen might lead.

The Right Tools for the Job

One problem men can face squarely is the selection of appropriate kitchen tools. Principal among these tools is the choice of quality pots and pans. Many men I know have been almost permanently turned off to learning how to cook because their first experiences with pots and pans were disastrous.

For example, I knew a guy—Kenny—recently divorced, who purchased a cheap new aluminum skillet every few days. The reason? All he knew how to do in the kitchen was open a can of corned beef hash, slop it into a skillet, turn the burner on high, and plop two eggs on top. He then covered this less-than-delectable mess with a dinner plate and waited for his concoction to smoke. Then he turned off the burner, removed the plate (usually burning his hand in the process) and ate the contents of the skillet down to the black. Yuck. At the end of this less than memorable meal, he discarded the skillet. Next day, along with antacids, he bought another one.

Kenny told me that he behaved this way because he did not know how to cook. I just stared at him. I asked him to show me his woodshop. Out there, in his space, I admitted that I didn't know my way around a wood shop.

He stared at me. "Well," he said, "that is probably because you never had anybody show you the right tools."

I smiled. "Exactly," I replied. "And neither have you in your own kitchen."

Later that day, I helped him invest in a set of quality cookware, a basic cookbook, and we went food shopping. With a few simple lessons, he moved from his burnt-skillet-a-day habit to culinary freedom. Last I heard, he had quite a local reputation as a gourmet.

Tooling Up

It can happen to you. Just as in anything else in this world, you must use the proper tool for the job. Never, ever, for any reason, purchase cheap cookware. There are two brands I recommend, although you may find others that fit the general criteria in your locale. These two brands are *Calphalon* and *Circulon*.* They are heavy, nonstick units that will seem pricey to you. On sale you can buy a basic set of Circulon pans, pots, and skillets for just under $200. Double that for Calphalon. But both brands last a long, long time. More importantly, they distribute heat evenly (important for everything you cook), contain moisture beautifully (essential for cooking rice and pastas), and clean easily. They also *really* look good.

Another must is to invest in a good quality matched set of kitchen knives (the substantial ones that come in a butcher block will do; remember, thickness in the blade and overall weight count—the heavier, the better) and cutting boards; display them on your countertop. When selecting knives, be honest with yourself about your abilities to actually sharpen the carbon steel models. If you can't do it and are unlikely to learn, then purchase a good set of stainless steel blades. When selecting a cutting board it is wise to buy two; one made out of heavy glass (to reserve for carving meats, which you can place in your dishwasher), another one made out of wood for veggies and cheeses.

Finally, purchase a reliable food processor, a hand-held electric mixer, and a quality electric blender. For the first and last items, I recommend Cuisinart products. Either store them on an available shelf in the kitchen or pantry, or if you have the room, display them on the countertop.

*No, they don't pay me for endorsing them. In fact, none of the
  specific brands I recommend in this book are paid endorsements.
  I recomend these products, because they are what I use and
  what I have found after years of cooking really do the job.

How Long Should I Keep It?

Clearing out your refrigerator is a good way to take stock of what you have, and what you really need or use. It also gives you an opportunity to apply this same reasoning to your relationships. Are you in a relationship that is long past its expiration date? Have certain aspects of your relationship become wilted? Why *are* you hanging on to that moldy and hairy stuff way back there?

Research indicates that most adults prefer to remain in unsatisfying relationships rather than face the possibility of having *no* relationship at all. Clean out your refrigerator and while you do think about your current and past relationships. Here are a few tips to guide you through the process:

Raw Material	Good For	Signs of Spoiling
Fresh leafy vegetables	3-5 days for most lettuces and spinach; cabbage; collard greens	Limpness in the leaves; yellow or brown spots; funky earthen smell, as in something that is about ready to return to its origins.
Vegetable side dish materials and stuff you would put in a decent salad	5-7 days for items like: asparagus; green beans; peas; snow peas; peppers (green, red, or yellow); mushrooms; zucchini; corn; celery; artichokes; avocados; tomatoes; cucumbers; alfalfa sprouts; etc. - you get the idea.	Limpness or soft spots; brown or black spots on surface (except avocados, which must be black to be ripe); slightly rotten smell.
Potatoes, carrots, and yellow, white, or red onions	Up to 4 months, if stored in a 40-50 degree Fahrenheit cool, dark place. If you are using a rack in your pantry, no longer than 1 month.	Soft spots on surfaces; brown or black spots; rotten smell.
Meat of any kind - chicken, port, beef	Check the package date and adhere to it as if your life depends on it, *which it does..*	If you ever open a package and it smells bad, *throw it away immediately*.

Now, what about your relationship? Asking yourself some basic questions can keep you from making the same mistakes again. Ask: What caused the spoilage? Lack of overt attention? Or inattention to detail? In both cases, diminished satisfaction with everyday exchanges of talk is likely to be at the center of it. Just "got tired of each other?" Or feel like "the spark has gone out" of your relationship? In both cases, you can add a few words to each cliché to locate the real problem. Got tired *of talking to* each other. The spark went out *of being with each other.* Again, the relationship has gone sour because you did not use the raw materials of words and actions to build something that could withstand the everyday tests of time.

Or are you looking in your emotional pantry and seeing a relationship that is at best half-empty? Now is the time to consider whether it is In need of just a few small improvements or adjustments to make it bloom into something really special, or is without hope of renewal? What can you learn from your past relationships? What are you going to do about it?

If you are unsatisfied, leaving things as they are can only mean that both of you are willing to settle for less than you deserve, or need. Is this how you want to live? If not, try applying a little imagination and playfulness to your relationship; put some fun back into being with each other! And if you really do try, and the fun and the spark just aren't forthcoming, then be a man. Explain how you feel to her. Don't lie. Don't hedge around the truth. And don't avoid talking about it. Be a man. I repeat, speak from your heart!

If there are signs of spoilage in your love life, there is never any better time than *now* to do something productive about it. Nothing that is rotten ever got rid of itself. If it comes to that, spend some time reflecting on what you can do to keep your relationships from going sour in the first place?

Why are Relationships Better in the Beginning?

The short answer is because you don't know each other very well yet. But short answers—like shortcuts in a recipe—though convenient, seldom produce excellence. And with this question there is a longer answer that better explains the issue.

The story of everyday American life is largely composed of beginnings and endings. Perhaps this is because as schoolchildren we are taught that history is marked by the beginnings and endings of wars; science is defined by discoveries and technologies by their final applications; business is about the making of deals and the signing of contracts; and law is summed up in the opening and closing arguments. In literature and film, particularly American literature and film, readers/ viewers have come to require dramatic beginnings and endings to define popu- lar as well as financial success. And, increasingly, in our relationships, we tend to be very good at creating imaginative and energetic beginnings and at surviving sudden, often tragic endings, but are less well suited for the everyday manage- ment and adaptability required for living through middles.

Why is this?

There are some obvious answers. First, in our culture we are attracted to and revere the experience of *newness.* But newness cannot, by definition, endure. Everything we didn't know about the other person, every aspect of her character, her intellect, her body, the stories of her life—once experienced as new can never be experienced as new again. Couples that fall apart often begin their casual drift away from each other when words they used to speak and find exciting, compelling, or just funny cease to be so. When the sex is no longer "what it once was."

When the magic is gone, and what is left behind *feels* like what has been left behind. When this happens, people say their relationship has become "stale," or "routine," or just "boring." In each of these terms there is the unspoken presence of its opposite: fresh, new, exciting.

If what we are experiencing in our relationship is informed, structured, by these terms, then we see how easy it is for us to be disappointed when the newness wears off and the "same old, same old" sets in. From a narrative perspective, we are no longer moving *toward* something, but *away* from it. What we have lacks the energy that anticipation establishes for us; what we see down the road is a further lessening of energy. What we fear when the newness is gone is our own death, due to unfulfilled causes.

A second reason for the appeal of a new relationship is that it awakens all of our senses. Mind and body rush together. We seem to feel more deeply, hold more closely, touch more gently, embrace more fully; the urgent blooming of a metaphorical Spring lives within our shared moment. Life happens to us. We find things brighter, more beautiful, funnier. We taste with greater relish. We hear things we never heard before. We sense the meanings of our new partner with a kind of eerie awareness, which is why so many new couples swear they feel as if they have known this new person all their lives!

> But, the beginning of romance, of love, like youth, is a fleeting promise that once spoken is gone forever. If we live for the moment of such youth, such newness, we are doomed to a life of multiple beginnings that never mature, and of multiple endings that increasingly seem inevitable.

A third reason—and probably the summary reason that informs the other two—is because our culture teaches us to produce and to consume, which is to say, to *value*, the purchase of the new over all other transactions. In part this is because commodity capitalism requires ever-expanding markets, and markets are dedicated to the singular proposition that all purchases must be rapidly repeated, including the purchases—the consumption—of experiences.

Everywhere we are surrounded by temptations that support our generalized cravings to consume, so much so that Kenneth Gergen, a social psychologist, says our selves are *saturated* with these images. Consider these common utterances as symptoms of this problem: We have closets full of clothes, but nothing to wear. Our two year-old car, although still stylish and running perfectly, no longer satisfies us. We feel that our computer, purchased just last season, needs to be upgraded. And so on.

All of these reasons—cultural, psychological, and economic—coalesce into a generalized desire for beginnings in all facets of our lives. Recognizing that this is true helps a little bit, but seldom affords any real resistance and never quenches our deep thirst for it. Given that we live under the spell of commodity capitalism and on the liquor of the always new—and those who don't usually want to—is it any wonder that our intimate relationships are often understood more by their beginnings and endings than by their middles?

Now you know why. The bigger question is what are you going to do about it?

OVERCOMING
SUPERMARKET DREAD

One of the unspoken reasons why men don't learn to

cook is that nobody ever taught us how to shop for

food. Upon entering a supermarket we are reduced to

one of two roles, both of which only prepare us for a

lifetime of kitchen idiocy.

Food Shopping Strategies

Option #1: Either we go in to pick up white bread, white milk, white eggs, and, by god, because we are MEN, cans of brown beer. Or, more often, Option #2, we just push the cart, pretending it is some sort of exotic vehicle and the aisles are our private raceway. If we are lucky, we get to check out the car or business magazines.

If you want to see genuine panic on the face of a man in a supermarket, just ask him what the difference is between extra virgin, and virgin, olive oils. Or get him to explain why it is that tomato paste is sold in those small cans. Or ask him what a chipotle is. In any of these scenarios, most men will respond with something like this: "Duh, I dunno." And then, they will become very interested in the white stuff in their cart.

I've often wished that supermarkets would follow the lead of super-sized hardware stores. Lowe's or Home Depot, for example, regularly offer free, short demonstrations or mini-course in activities such as "building a deck" or "installing automatic lawn sprinklers." Guys come. Supermarkets could offer "selecting fresh vegetables," or "the basics of spicing." Maybe if they offered free food, guys would attend these sessions in droves.

The problem is that men thrive on being basic. Supermarkets, especially these days, offer too many choices. This has a profound and negative effect on males. As the choices of available food options expand, the contents of our shopping carts are proportionately reduced. It is as if the complexity of decision-making about food inspires a rebellion against making *any* decisions.

So, we just go with what we know. All oil is oil, right? Tomato paste, tomato puree, diced tomatoes, what's the difference? Who cares? Hey, if it can't be eaten between two slices of Wonder Bread what good is it anyway?

Sentiments of this sort always remind me of the wisdom of Jennifer James. A former anthropologist, she lectures on the facts of social evolution. She points out that in each of the four great eras of human evolution—cave dwellers, hunter-gatherers, agricultural, and mass production—there were those persons who refused to learn the new understandings and skills associated with the engines of change. The result was that those who refused to change stopped evolving and eventually died off.

We are now living at the dawn of the fifth great era of human evolution—the information age. As I mentioned earlier, women's and men's social and family roles have been significantly altered; so too has our way of organizing understandings of, and learning and/or adapting new skills to, those alterations. Those men who are evolving with the times are learning how to think about, and do, things that our forefathers would not have considered "natural," or even "appropriate. " But our forefathers are gone. We are here. The future is ours.

Now this may seem like a large way of introducing how to overcome your lack of skill when entering a supermarket. But the larger circles that define the seemingly smaller and more localized meanings of life are always there, and our ability to connect our daily experiences to them is critically important. So what should a guy do when entering a supermarket? How should he prepare for the experience of food shopping? What are the hazards to avoid, or the secrets to acquire? What would constitute a successful shopping experience?

Your Best Defense - The List

The best strategy for overcoming supermarket dread is to know what you are going to buy before you get there. First, *make a list.* The list is your Saturday morning mission statement that contains the core values of your basic game plan. As such, your shopping list should contain all of the components of a strategy to get you through the experience; it should also be flexible enough to accommodate unexpected opportunities. Again, one of the lessons acquired from the changes in business wrought by the global information age is the need to focus on what needs to be done to accomplish your mission, while being open to unforeseen possibilities. When you shop for food, you are engaging in a business transaction that mirrors and reflects the diversity of the global marketplace. You should bring to that transaction all of the skills you would bring to any other business transaction.

What should be on your shopping list? This question challenges every consumer, everyday.

Many men believe, however, that the mystery of what appears on a shopping list is one to which only women hold the key. Imagine what the world would be like if this same illogical conclusion were used to block men's understanding of strategic planning! In fact, women who are smart food shoppers practice many of the skills of strategic planners: women imagine the future with their needs in it, they organize those needs in manageable ways, they evaluate the options for satisfying those needs, they treat the purchase of foodstuffs as the strategic acquisition of new resources, and they deploy those resources to enrich the family's experiential profits. Men should do exactly the same thing.

Overcoming Supermarket Dread

To make a strategic plan-oriented shopping list, perform the following steps, *in order:*

1. Determine whether you are shopping for *one meal*, for a *weekend* of eating, or for a *week* of living and dining in your home.

2. If you are shopping for one *meal*, find the appropriate recipe, check the contents of your refrigerator and pantry, and derive your list of needs from what is absent from your home.

3. If you are shopping for a *weekend*, organize the contents of your shopping list in a way that truly reflects your lifestyle. Do you really eat three meals a day? Or do you eat something sweet for breakfast, skip lunch, have a middle of the afternoon snack, and then look forward to a nutritionally balanced evening meal? Do any of the meals you are planning have a strong likelihood of leftovers? If so, do you plan to freeze them (in order to take to work for lunch next week) or eat them as part of a snack the following day? How many people are you likely to see over the weekend, and how many of them will be offered food?

4. If you are planning food shopping for a *week*, follow the same steps in (a) for the meals you plan to make, and in (b) for the lifestyle add-ons, but also include basic necessities such as dishwashing and hand soap, cleaning agents, paper products, liquid refreshments, and the like.

5. Organize your list for a manageable experience.

Write out your list in a way that corresponds to the floorplan of the supermarket. If you cannot buy everything you need at one location, use separate pieces of paper for each planned stop.

6. Evaluate the available options.

Is what you plan to purchase on sale? Is there a long-term strategic advantage in stocking up on non-perishable items, such as frozen food or canned goods? Are one bag of tortilla chips and the leftover salsa in the fridge likely to feed the usual gang that stops over after the tennis match? Is one bottle of wine really ever enough for a romantic evening? These questions should be derived from your experiences and informed by a healthy respect for the fact that most of us have pantries stocked with things we will never use, refrigerators with foodstuffs that will rot before we can eat them. In most cases our overstocked but under-used food items were acquired because we failed to match our shopping lists to our realistic needs. My advice: examine your pantry for evidence of bad shopping deci-sions and donate the canned or unopen, unexpired errors to the next local food drive so that someone else can benefit from your mistakes. And most important, learn from your mistakes.

Second, *organize your list by food category.* The categories should corre-spond to your likely passage through the various areas of the supermarket. In other words, if you always enter the store through the same doors and find yourself in the fresh produce section, the first section of your list should include items likely to be found there: salad greens, fresh veggies, and an array of fruits. If you then pass by the deli, your list should reflect that.

If you need canned goods, all of the items likely to be found in the canned good sections should appear on the same place on your list. Dairy items are found in the last aisle—good, let your list show that. And so on.

This simple shopping strategy saves time and money, and allows you to work your list as well as you would a business plan. You will walk through the aisles of the supermarket as a man with a mission to accomplish, which is to say that you will look like someone who knows what he is doing.

> Many men approach time spent in a supermarket as if it were time spent in prison: the shorter the sentence, the better. As a result, we often misrepresent the time needed to do a good job of shopping, and increase the frustration level considerably.

By contrast, I advise beginning with the lessons of your experiences as a casual walker. How long does it take you to walk a mile at a leisurely pace, with some quality time built in for admiring the roses? Thirty minutes? Forty-five? An hour? Now consider that most weekly shopping trips in one of today's mega-markets comprise at least a half-mile walk, often impeded by other shoppers, and generally delayed for a minimum of ten additional minutes at the check-out line. By the time you add in time spent walking to and from your vehicle, time unloading your bags from the cart into the vehicle, and the driving time to and from the market itself, you have a fair estimate of how long this experience should take.

It is also important to allow enough time to compare the quality and prices of items on your list. Here again, most men—and increasingly, many women—just buy whatever label falls readily to hand, and roughly corresponds to what they want. *Lemme outta here*!

In the global marketplace, this obvious and observable fact would quickly lead manufacturers and salespersons to offer the highest priced products at hand-and-eye level, which, in fact, is precisely what food stores do. Their profits increase, and you complain about how much $100 at the market doesn't buy anymore. Duh, I wonda why? Learn to look up and down, and all around, for bargains. If it helps, think of it as a 360-degree audit.

A Practical Guide to Speaking in Supermarkets

Men often view the experience of shopping as if it were analogous to walking through a hospital or public library, where the watchword is always: Silence! Tight-lipped, usually under-informed, and generally uncomfortable with shopping rituals, these otherwise worldly men fear asking important questions of persons and/or personnel who can help them. When these under-experienced, non-talkers do speak, it is usually to give loud voice to some vaguely inarticulate and largely moronic complaint, addressed to some unseen but all-knowing Supermarket God: "Chissakes, why the hell are the damned eggs always all the way over here!?!"

As with any display of lunacy in public, the otherwise helpful supermarket personnel and most of the other patrons will identify you as nuts, dismiss your words as the blathering of an idiot, and remember your face, *forever.*

My experiences as a shopper have taught me some basic lessons about speaking in food stores. Just as in any service-oriented business, it is wise to offer a friendly greeting to supermarket employees prior to making a request or asking a question. It is also a good idea to treat them as competent profes-sionals, and become known as a person who regularly spends money here, appreciates quality at a fair price, and rewards good service, even when all that is called for is a simple word of thanks.

Overcoming Supermarket Dread

There is a lot to be gained from developing a positive working relationship with the fish market supervisor, including tips on which size of shrimp are best for the meal you plan to prepare. Ditto for the deli workers, or produce employees. Always be friendly to—and respectful of—checkout employees and baggers. Trust me, they will remember only those persons who treat them well and those who treat them poorly.

Finally, two small but useful pieces of advice from Dr. Bud's storehouse of practical information for male food shoppers. First, when you don't know where to find an item, *ask*. This has no perceptible negative affect on your manhood, but it does mark you as a person who is not afraid of his own voice in a store. The goal is to accomplish your mission; never forget that. To locate the desired item in a timely fashion, avoid wandering around lost in the store. If this has the added benefit of encouraging you to learn how to ask for directions while driving, so much the better.

Second, do not fear fresh, canned, or frozen items that are not grown, harvested, or manufactured in the good ol' US-of-A. Unfortunately, many otherwise competent global businessmen's approach to purchase of imported goods if it were an overt betrayal of our country. Then, in a frantic search to prove their loyalty, they grab the first can that is wrapped in a familiar, American label. Too bad, really. In many cases the price of these goods is higher, and, if the man in question would simply read the label, chances are good he would find that he is buying the same product—it is grown, harvested, and/or manufactured overseas and simply marketed through the American firm. Your misplaced loyalty is really only to the middleman.

If you are worried about your health and safety from overseas bacterial agents or germs, please be assured that all foodstuffs that come into our beloved country must pass the same governmental muster as food grown, manufactured, or produced here. The point is, however, to abandon your misplaced prejudices and broaden your international food horizons.

Finally, think about the fact that if you plan to prepare a Korean, Mexican, Italian, or—although this is unlikely, a British—dish, chances are good that something created by knowledgeable and experienced workers in that country of origin probably are at least more authentic, if not better, than the copy of the product made here. Learn to evaluate your options by comparing ingredients, prices, and shelf-expiration dates.

To become a knowledgeable and smart shopper is to become a strategic planner in this sphere of your life. Not only will your ability to save time and money improve, your overall enjoyment of the shopping experience will too.

WOOING HER

Courtship should not end when you have

established an enduring relationship. The true

courtier understands that his must be a lifelong

commitment to communication excellence,

and to continue, in all manner of worldly things,

to be worthy of her love and support.

Men often believe that true communication with women is a mystery. The age-old question "What do women want?" is widely acknowledged to be both inevitable and unanswerable. Why? Well, popular books point out women and men act as if we are from different planets, or are at least psychologically and linguistically derived from opposing cultures. Authors and talk show hosts tell us that men and women "speak different languages" and that, in relationships, we make mistakes, hurt each other's feelings, or fail to communicate because we do not share the same assumptions about the meanings for words and actions. Recent self-help literature stresses the fact that most men do not listen well, nor do many of us know how to engage in meaningful talk with women about our goals, needs, anxieties, or ideals of relational happiness.

> Given this news, the future of women and men together seems bleak. But there is hope. Communication research provides a few good ideas that can help us turn the corner. One of these "good ideas" is the age-old wisdom—first articulated by Baldassare Castiglione in the classic work *The Book of the Courtier*—that advises men who seek to advance their interests through courtship to adhere to this singular communication principle: *Adapt your messages to your listener.*

This means to think about how what you plan to say might be taken by the specific person you are saying it to. To take into account her unique needs. Her personal desires. Her known interpretations of persons and things.

You should also learn to:

1. Avoid asserting your authority when you know that is likely to set her off. In other words, don't just assume you have all the answers. *Listen* for a change, let her talk.

2. Develop a sense of humor and be fun to be around. No one—man, woman, or child—wants to be around someone who is only focused on work or tasks and doesn't know how to have fun.

3. Be mindful of what she considers appropriate in all circumstances. If you are having dinner with her family be on your best behavior. And, occasionally, be on your best behavior *when it is just the two of you.* This means no offensive noise of any type. Need I say more?

4. Respect her feelings, her intuitions, her views. And, if she feels you respect her, she will in turn respect you. See how this works?

5. Dress for her, as she often does for you. Would you want to sit down to dinner and have to look at the t-shirt you are wearing right now? When was the last time you splashed on a little cologne *at the end of the day, just for her.* Come on guys! This is your woman we are talking about.

6. Develop yourself in all intellect and skill categories, as a sign of your intention to constantly improve, to be a lifelong learner, to more fully evolve as a man and as a person. How many conversations can you expect her to sit through about the revolutionary new sales technique for the XXXYY you developed, or the best Knick's, Laker's, UNC game ever, or the fact that the garage just can't seem to get your car right? Need help here? Read on.

Developing Your Rhetorical Flexibility

The linguist Deborah Tannen writes about misunderstandings in relationships by demonstrating how differently women and men use and interpret the
meanings of words. What she found is that women and men tend to live
within their own worlds of meaning which create differences, and that gender
is the single most important ingredient in understanding those differences.

Mostly, she is right. Most people, most of the time, are less mindful about
their communication practices than they are about the weather (despite the
fact that we can change one and not the other). And, it is also true that
many men and women behave in ridiculously rigid ways. Regardless of
gender, we assume that the way we see and interpret the world is pretty
much the only way to do it. We also assume that whatever attitudes, values,
and beliefs we have grown up respecting must be the "right" ones. Hence,
when boy meets girl and both of us assume that how we are listening and
speaking, as well as how we are making sense of the world, is the one right
way, we tend to miscommunicate. We speak *to*, but not *with* each other.

So what can we do? How can we improve?

> In addition to understanding that men and women
> communicate differently, we must also work to be-
> come better communicators. Simply "knowing"
> there are differences doesn't mean we will
> communicate better. To do that requires work.

Communication scholars believe that one way to work toward communication excellence is to practice the skills of *rhetorical flexibility*. Think of it this
way: To get your body in shape you need to become more flexible, so you do
stretching exercises To become rhetorically flexible means to practice your
ability to adapt your messages to the needs and expectations of your listeners. In short, this means exercising your mind, your mouth, and your body in
ways that are designed to improve the responses you get from others to what
you say and do.

Wooing Her

Here are six ways for you to practice this important skill:

Responsiveness

This skill refers to your ability to listen to what is being said and respond to it meaningfully. The relevant questions for you to consider include:

> Do you listen to your partner? *Really* listen?
>
> Do you pay close attention to her communication needs and goals? To her anxieties and fears?
>
> Do you *respond* to her in complete sentences, rather than just say "uh-huh," or "okay," or "sure"?
>
> Do you *respect* her needs and goals, or simply assume that whatever she is saying is probably less important than whatever you are thinking about? Are you mindful of the need to be responsive at times other than when you want something from her, such as a favor, money, or sex?

Flexibility

This skill refers to your need for control, and your ability to change your role or plans to meet her needs. The relevant questions for you to consider include:

> Do you find that you need to always be in charge, or are you willing to do what she wants to do at least as often as you expect her to do what you want to do?
>
> Are you willing to alter or change your communication practices to meet her needs?
>
> Are you willing to change your plans, just because she asks you to?

Do you find that you are you are always saying pretty much the same things when you speak to each other? If so, perhaps you need to work on becoming more flexible in your choice of language, communication topics, and the balance of power that defines your relationship.

Adaptiveness

This skill is derived from the fact that most close relationships require us to respond meaningfully to emerging contingencies and to live with and within life's many sources of ambiguity. The relevant questions for you to consider include:

Are you willing to do this?

Are you willing to live with the stress and strain of everyday adjustments to your schedule, your rituals, your preferences?

Can you become the sort of man who lives within each moment fully, regardless of where it leads you or what happens in it, rather than one that rigidly depends upon an exact sequence of events and episodes for relational satisfaction?

Purposefulness

This skill is based on the idea that most communication in relationships should be goal-oriented because your partner will respond to it as if it is. The relevant questions for you to consider include:

Do you know what it would take, in your relationship, to make you happy? How about her? If you don't, how will you be able to determine if this is the relationship you need to be in? Or what you could do to help make it that way? If you do know what makes you happy, then you can use goals to guide your choice of talk, your selection of actions, and as a way of improving your chances of getting there.

Do you engage in relational talk "mindfully" or "mindlessly"? Although most of our everyday interactions with strangers, coworkers, and peers can be described as relatively "mindless" because we "just yak" or exchange small talk, our talk with relational partners needs to be more mindful. This means we ought to speak more often with a clear goal for the outcome of the talk in mind.

Why?

Two reasons. First, because your partner will assume you have one (if you didn't, there would be little point in talking to you at all, right?). Second, relational satisfaction is largely based on our everyday sense of happiness, and our everyday sense of happiness is often internally measured by our ability to feel as if, on a daily basis, we are reaching our relational goals.

Rational

This skill is based on the fact that although we like—and even seek—novelty in a relationship, we also expect a level of predictability in our partner. We want our significant others to richly inhabit a centered place in our lives, where "centered" means rational, orderly, understandable. For most people, "rational" is defined not only by not acting "out of character," or doing crazy, reckless things; it is defined by spoken words, commitments, promises, goals, and values that build predictable, comfortable routines and roles into daily life. You expect her to behave rationality, which means to act within the boundaries of what has been uttered and should be honored between you. There is only one relevant question for you to consider here:

> Can she expect *you* to live up to your promises, keep your word, honor your obligations, and do what you say you will do?

Responsibility

This skill is comes from the idea that your character is largely determined by your actions and your words. The relevant questions for you to consider include:

> Do you take responsibility for your words? For your actions?

> Do you know when and how to admit you were wrong, and acknowledge it in your heart? To say you are sorry, and really mean it? More importantly, are you willing to *learn* from your relational transgressions and mistakes? To live at least a little bit above what you think you can get away with?

These six skills can help you think about your communicative shortcomings and show you productive ways to change for the better.

Dr. Bud's Guide to Setting a Table

Women do not like to have a fine meal served on paper plates with plastic spoons. Nor do they think a paper towel is a good substitute for a proper napkin. They appreciate the little things, such as a well-presented meal on a well-ordered table. For this reason, let's review the *basics*.

- Each person who is seated at the table should have a centered place setting in front of her or him. The plates should match, so too should the silverware and glasses.

- To the right of the plate should be placed the folded cloth napkin, a knife, and one or two spoons, depending on the meal.

- To the left should be placed two forks (one shorter one for salads, the taller one for the main course).

- If you are serving soup, place the soupspoon (and don't use a regular spoon, you lout!) at the top of the placing setting, just about an inch north of the plate.

- If you are serving salad, place the salad plate either on top of the main course dish, or to the right and north of the knife and spoons.

- If you want to use a bread plate, that one should be placed north of the forks.

- Water glasses go slightly to the right of the salad plate, and if you are serving wine (and who wouldn't?), the wineglass should be placed to the right of the water glass.

- Sea-salt and mixed peppercorn grinders (yes, dammit, grinders) should be in the middle of the table, within easy reach of both of you.

Music is almost always a good companion to a well-served meal. Musical tastes vary considerably, so I'll forgo my usual advice here, which would be (if you are wondering), light jazz played softly.

Here are some common "guy things" that you must avoid if you are to make a good impression. First and foremost, no untoward bodily noises—of any kind or from any place of origin—are necessary or funny during the preparation, serving, or eating of the meal. If you feel an urgent need that cannot be properly suppressed, excuse yourself and go to the bathroom or outside.

Second, how and what you serve the meal on matters. Do not serve soup in measuring cups, vegetables in the pan you prepared them in, or deliver meats to the table with your fingers. Invest in a matched set of serving plates and bowls. Trust me on this.

Third, avoid eating one thing at a time. Exercise diversity in your dining pleasure. Women notice this and it symbolizes something; I don't know what, exactly, but there it is. The exceptions to this rule are (1) to finish your salad or soup prior to the main course, and (2) the main course prior to dessert. Some Europeans prefer to eat the salad after the main course, but unless you have always done it this way, don't start. Your eyes will give you away, and will look foolish.

> Fourth, don't ask for or expect your guest (even if she is your wife) to do the dishes. You invited her, remember. This is not about balance, it is not about power, and it is not about dividing roles according to some tribal ritual. As host, you should remove the dishes. You do not have to do them right away, unless the conversation at dinner convinced you that you'd be better off doing the dishes than furthering your chances.

Fifth, and finally, don't drink wine from the bottle, ever. Okay, in bed, maybe, but never at the table.

Timing is Everything

Nothing and nobody respects timing as much as cooking and women do. There are obvious reasons why a woman would. If I have to spell it out for you, probably you should be reading a very different kind of guidebook right now.

Anyway, cooking is very much a matter of timing. For this reason, I have tried to explain precisely how long each part of the cooking process should take for each of my recipes. This is another good reason not to deviate from my instructions. There is nothing so disappointing as to have the sauce "just right" long before the meat is ready, if you follow my meaning here. The same thing is true for timing veggies, pastas, and so on.

Timing, however, is at least as much a *contextual* as a linear concept. This means that no matter how long—in linear minutes—something should take according to the instructions, the more overriding concern is for how it works as a measuring device within the contexts and purposes of its use. For this reason, I have included both ways of telling time in my recipes—first, by linear measurement and second by what you should be able to tell, by sight, smell, or feel, when an appropriate length of time has passed to ensure the proper result.

Okay, guys, that's pretty much all of it. We've covered all of those things you've always wanted to know about shopping, about kitchens, about recipes, and about serving the meal. We are now ready to act on what we have learned.

Let's *cook*!

THE RECIPES

The Cooking Process

You wouldn't begin a project at work without a plan, nor should you cook without one. Most men forget this principle when they enter a kitchen. Too bad. Cooking is a lot like managing a project: plan your work, and work your plan.

Stage one of the process is choosing a meal and selecting the appropriate recipes. Stage two is making a shopping list for the items you will need to follow the recipes. Stage three is following the recipes to their natural conclusion. Stage four is serving the meal. Stage five is enjoying it. Stage six depends on who you are with and whether or not you believe, in your heart of hearts, that the dishes have to be done right away. Let's examine each of these stages in more detail.

Planning a meal requires a bit of skill. You need to have some idea of the vegetables that go with the meat you are serving. Would salad be good? Or, would it be overkill? In this book, I've laid out entire meals for you, with some flexible options once you've acquired the basic idea. Keep it simple, fella. Just choose one.

Once you've selected the meal, simply follow the recipes. If you come this far, I'm sure you can do this. You should be, too. However, there is one thing I will caution you about, because it is a common problem among guys and can get in the way of accomplishing this otherwise pretty simple task. You have to give up being in control, at least for awhile. You will need to do what I say, in the order I advise. No deviations, please. Surrender to the recipe.

Organize all of the resources you will need to accomplish your goal. In the recipe section of this book you will see the following headings for each recipe:

Raw Materials

Tools

The Blueprint

Before you begin cooking, make a list of the ingredients for each menu item: the appetizer, the main dish, the side dishes, the salad, and the dessert. Develop a plan for preparing and cooking the items required for each menu item. Ask yourself:

> How long does it take to assemble the ingredients?
>
> How long does it take prepare (e.g., chopping, cutting, measuring, etc.)
>
> How long does each menu item need to cook?
>
> What order should they be in to make sure everything gets done on schedule?

Use this column to see if downtime between tasks exists; for example, waiting for water to come to a boil usually provides enough time to prepare veggies for sautéing, create a light appetizer, or assemble a dessert. It is important to allow a little room for error in your calculations, so build in an extra 10-15 minutes overall. Most cooks fail because they don't plan! There is nothing worse than spending an hour in the kitchen and ending up with a big mess and nothing to eat. A few minutes of planning up front will ensure this doesn't happen to you and that you *both* enjoy the fruits of your labor.

SANDWICHES FOR TWO

"She interrupted her labors long enough to construct a

towering Dagwood for me. Thick slices of sour rye

served as bookends, and the literature within included

slices of smoked turkey, beefsteak tomato, and

Bermuda onion: all with a healthy dollop of Ursi's

homemade mayo containing a jolt of Dijon mustard. I

carried this masterpiece up to my suite, silently giving

thanks to John Montagu, 4th Earl of Sandwich."

—Lawrence Sanders, <u>McNally's Puzzle</u>

The Weekend Sandwich

"Doing lunch" has become such an expected ritual of the work week that lunch itself is worn out. Everyone I know either bags it (usually yogurt, carrot sticks, and bottled water), nukes it (usually something from *Healthy Choice* or *Budget Gourmet*), or walks a couple of blocks downtown to the nearest Thai or Indian place for the special. Nothing wrong with any of these options. As is true with so much of what we take for granted, it's seldom what we are doing now that is a problem; instead, it is what we have *forgotten* how to do, or simply don't do anymore.

One of the lost arts of the American lunch is the sandwich. The *weekend* sandwich. True, you can go a decent deli almost anywhere and order what you want. But the fact is nothing tastes quite like homemade, nor lends itself to such spontaneous creativity.

Why have we lost the art of making our own sandwich? In part, it is because of the intrusion of the demands of the work week into our everyday luncheon routines. Unless a deli is close-by, or delivers, a luncheon sandwich must be prepared prior to leaving for work. Now, even the best-intentioned sandwich, at seven a.m., created with top ingredients, and stored in a plastic container designed for the purpose, by noon will be a cold sopping disgrace. And besides, most people are just too busy to take the time to make a good sandwich before leaving for work.

For this reason, I recommend reserving the making and enjoyment of sandwiches for the weekend. The weekend sandwich should be conceptualized as an alternative to whatever it is that you bag, nuke, or order out during the week. It should be viewed not as "just a sandwich," but as a minor culinary opportunity. Like the character Dagwood in the comic strip *Blondie*, the weekend sandwich man is a man fully capable of placing between two slices of good bread a veritable feast. I begin with two relatively simple-to-assemble weekend sandwiches and end with some advice about small talk. I think you'll be surprised how similar the two are.

Sandra's Choice

The basic sandwich is a vegetarian's delight, made for the first time by me for my lovely wife, Sandra. Do not be mislead by the gentleness of this sandwich. As I explain later, it is the basis for all good sandwiches. By mastering the basics, you open the door to possibility.

Raw Materials

1 freshly baked round of crusty bread, such as: Seven Grain, Herb, Sunflower Seed, or Russian Pumpernickel

½ pint of fresh radish or alfalfa sprouts

½ sliced avocado, skin and pit removed

¼ red bell pepper, rinsed and sliced into thin strips

¼ lb Italian Cremini mushrooms, cleaned and very thinly sliced

½ fresh tomato, rinsed and thickly sliced

Mayonnaise

Dried basil, to taste

¼ - ½ of a Vidalia onion, sliced any way you want it (optional)

Tools

Cutting Board

Serrated Knife (the longer one in the set, with the jagged edge)

Sharp Knife

The Blueprint

1. Using a serrated knife, cut two slices of bread ¼" thick.

2. Spread the Mayo on both slices of the bread.

3. Sprinkle about ¼ teaspoon of dried basil leaves into the Mayo.

4. Line a side of the bread with a layer of sprouts.

5. Add, in order: sliced tomato, sliced avocado (see "On Avocados"), sliced mushrooms, sliced red pepper, the (optional) sliced onion.

6. Cut in half; serve on a plate with your favorite chips and a Kosher dill pickle.

Dr. Bud's Smoked Turkey and Avocado Sandwich

This is the meatier version of the sandwich described above.

Add to the Sandra's Choice sandwich, between steps 3 and 4, ¼ - ½ lb of thin-sliced mesquite-smoked turkey. Delete the sprouts and (maybe) the sliced mushrooms. The onion is no longer optional, and for any self-respecting guy should be sliced thick. Add a piece of any green leafy lettuce (not Iceberg!) before you close the sandwich.

You can add a thick slice of provolone cheese, if you can stand the fat. I often do, and then spend an extra half-hour at the gym the next day.

Some people may prefer to use a Dijon-style mustard in place of the Mayo-and-basil mix. In my opinion this works best if you make the sandwich with regular turkey, smoked turkey, or even Virginia-baked ham. When *mesquite*-flavored meat is used, however, the mustard tends to obscure the mesquite.

On Avocados

Many males I know eschew avocados unless they are disguised in guacamole. This is an unfortunate and unnecessary habit. Is it yours? If so, I suspect there are two reasons for this avoidance of one of nature's tastiest veggies (1) no one has taught you how to select an avocado, and (2) no one has taught you how to peel one. Allow me to remedy these symptoms in the greater cause of freeing you to use this attractive and delicious addition to many sandwiches and salads.

Select only dark green-to-black skinned avocados. That's pretty simple. The medium green ones are immature, where "immature" means "a bad thing." Most any dark green-to-black avocado will do, but the best ones give in slightly to the touch without being too mushy. As with most things in life, the larger ones are not necessarily better. They generally have larger pits, as well.

To peel an avocado requires that you:

1. Slice gently through the outside layer of skin lengthwise, to the pit, from top to bottom (all the way around).

2. Twist the two halves in opposite directions.

3. Remove the pit.

4. Using your fingers, not a knife, peel back the outside layer in a circular manner. It's a little odd to begin with, but with some practice gets easier.

Taking it to the Next Level

Once you've gotten used to the idea of experimenting with ingredients for a weekend sandwich, you can begin experimenting with its *form*. Form, in this sense, means the very idea of it, from its shape to its contents.

For this reason, I want you to consider the concept of a California Roll (and the Tortilla Roll-up) as a logical extension to the basic form of the weekend sandwich. You basically have something tasty inside something else intended to hold it together, much as bread does for a sandwich or "hi" and "bye" do for a conversation.

California Rolls are an easy sandwich alternative taught to me by our friend Elizabeth Taggart. They can serve as either a wonderful appetizer or along with Spinach Sides and Cold Cucumbers Salad as a full-fledged meal. I prefer serving this sushi-based feast with veggies and cooked shrimp or crabmeat. You may opt for raw fish, but I wouldn't recommend it. Genuine sushi chefs get paid well because they know what they are doing and their customers don't drop dead after they eat. Remember, you are a beginner.

I've organized these recipes in the exact order I want you to do them in. The point is to show you how really easy it is *when you follow instructions*.

Spinach Sides

The left-overs from this side dish can also be used in the California Rolls described below. Or, you can serve this as a side dish with many chicken, pork, or steak main courses.

Sandwiches for Two

Raw Materials

1 bag of spinach; shredded with the stems removed

1 clove of garlic

2 teaspoons of sesame oil

1 Tablespoon of soy sauce

1 teaspoon of toasted sesame seeds (buy them toasted)

green onions

Tools

large pot

knife

small mixing bowl

serving bowl

The Blueprint

1. Bring a large pot of cold water to a boil.

2. Added the shredded spinach.

3. Blanch (e.g., place the spinach in the boiling water for 1 minute, just until the spinach begins to cook).

4. Drain the spinach by squeezing it between sheets of paper towel until most of the water is gone. This process leaves you with a small lump of spinach.

5. Place the drained spinach in a serving bowl.

6. Add 1 clove of garlic, thinly sliced and chopped. (Thin here means really thin, as thin as you can slice it.)

7. Mix the sesame oil, sesame seeds, and soy sauce together in the small mixing bowl.

8. Add the dressing to the spinach. Toss until completely mixed.

9. Cover with plastic wrap and refrigerate for 15-30 minutes.

Cold Cucumber Salad

This is a great warm weather dish. It can also be served as side dish for many main courses.

Raw Materials

2-3 small cucumbers

2 Tablespoons Sushinoko (dried vinegar, available at Oriental markets)*

1 clove of garlic, thinly sliced

* Don't be intimidated by the items on these lists that can only be found at the Oriental market. Almost every good size town has at least one and I have found shopping there to be quite pleasant. If you can't pronounce something, just take this book and point. The shopkeeper will help you and I think you will find it is well worth the extra effort.

Tools

cutting board

sharp knife

shallow serving dish

The Blueprint

1. Rinse and cut off the ends of the cucumbers. You can peel the cucumbers or leave the skins on, either way is fine.

2. Slice the cucumber into very thin round slices.

3. Arrange in a thin layer on the serving dish.

4. Sprinkle with the dried vinegar.

5. Stir.

6. Cover with plastic wrap and refrigerate for 15-30 minutes, until cold.

California Rolls

These are easy to make and quite impressive. And, because you cut them into bit size pieces, you can feed each other if the mood strikes.

Raw Materials

2 cup Nishiki rice (This is an Oriental, medium-grain sticky rice. If you can't find it, try the Oriental market.)

4 cups water

Nori wrappers (these are the seaweed wrappers that hold the rolls together)

1 medium-sized cucumber

½ red pepper

½ Daikon (This is an Oriental staple that can be found in the refrigerator section of the Oriental market. Or, as Sandra has discovered, bread 'n' butter pickles work just as well.)

½ avocado

crab meat from the fresh fish section of your market

Tools

Rice Steamer or Large Pot

sharp knife

2 cutting boards (one for cutting, one for rolling)

rice paddle or wooden spoon

The Blueprint

The optimal way to prepare the rice for this dish is in a rice steamer. If you don't have a rice steamer, and you love rice, then invest in one. I just bought one this year and I love it. It is amazing how much time it saves and how much better rice prepared this way tastes. If you only plan to cook rice occasionally, then you can get away with using ye old standard pot with a tight fitting lid.

If you are using a rice steamer:

1. Fill the pan of the steamer with 4 cups of water and 2 cups of rice.

2. Turn the steamer on and wait until the rice is done.

If you are using a pot on the stove:

1. Fill the pan with 4 cups of cold water.

2. Bring to a boil.

3. Add the rice.

4. Cover and reduce the heat to low.

5. Wait 20 minutes. The rice should be flufly and sticky with no water remaining in the pan. Move on to step six while the rice is cooking.

6. Prepare the cucumber by washing it with cold water, peeling it, cutting it lengthwise and removing the seed sections. Slice into strips, a little larger than the size of a pencil.

7. Prepare the red pepper by washing it with cold water, cutting it in half, removing the seed section in the center and all the loose seeds and slicing it into thin strips. You can use the red pepper just like this or you can sauté it in ½ teaspoon sesame oil. All this means is you put the sesame oil in a skillet on the stove, over medium heat. You add the red pepper and stir around until the pepper is warm but not totally wilted.

8. Prepare the Daikon (or Bread 'n' Butter pickles) by slicing it into thin strips.

9. Prepare the avocado. See the section *On Avocados.*

10. Prepare the crab meat by cutting it into thin slices.

11. Pour the steamed rice into a large bowl. Add 1 Tablespoon of Sushinoko (dried vinegar) to 4 cups of cooked rice. Stir thoroughly while rice is still warm. Allow rice to cool before making rolls.

12. Place a Nori wrapper, shiny side down, rough side up on the cutting board you are using for rolling.

13. Put about ¼ cup of rice in the center of the wrapper.

14. Gently smooth out the rice until it coats the wrapper, making sure you get the edges. Don't try to press down to flatten the rice, you want it to remain fluffy.

15. About one third of the way up from the bottom edge of the wrapper, lay a strip of avocado, cucumber, red pepper, and Daikon.

16. Add the crabmeat.

17. Start rolling from the bottom. Tightly fold the bottom part of the roll *over* the vegetables. The first roll should seal the ingredients in place. Continue to roll, tightening the roll as you go. The first two or three you do will not be great, but you will get the hang of it pretty quickly. You might want to practice your technique before you plan to serve this dish.

18. Cut the roll into 1/2 inch slices.

19. Arrange on a serving dish and serve with the accompaniments described below.

Some like it Hot Sauce

California rolls should be served with a small portion of ginger and a small bowl of soy sauce. You can also serve Wasabi (available at the Oriental market). But be warned, Wasabi is HOT! The sauces below are a variation on the Wasabi theme.

WASABI DIPPING SAUCE (medium hot)

¼ clove garlic, sliced thin

3 Tablespoons low-sodium soy sauce

½ teaspoon Wasabi paste.

Mix ingredients with fork.

KILLER WASABI DIPPING SAUCE (hot hot)

2 Tablespoons soy sauce

4 Tablespoons rice vinegar

¼ clove garlic, thinly sliced

1 - 2 teaspoons Wasabi paste

4-6 shakes of the hot red sesame oil

Mix thoroughly and don't say I didn't warn you . . .

See how easy this is?

You can vary the veggies and try other combinations. You can use cooked shrimp instead of crab. Think of a California Roll as a roll-up-style sandwich and use your imagination! Here are some other options. Instead of using a Nori wrapper:

- use a soft tortilla. Warm the tortilla before filling (follow package instructions). Instead of using veggies, use smoked turkey with jalapena cream cheese and a little red salsa.

- use a pita. Fill it with whatever you like. Try hummus and alfalfa sprouts. Or thin strips of curried beef or chicken.

With either option, you can serve the rolls whole or slice into 1" pieces before serving. Suddenly, the idea of a sandwich seems far more satisfying than it did when you began this chapter, doesn't it? See what a little effort, and a little imagination, can do?

Of Sandwiches and Small Talk

What I've tried to do in this opening chapter is show you how to improve your ability to make a tasty sandwich by taking some minor risks with the basic ingredients. This is also a metaphor for improving your small talk with women.

Conversation between women and men should not rely solely on basic, ordinary, and everyday exchanges of surface pleasantries. This would be like eating fast food cheeseburgers for lunch everyday, and thinking your diet is healthy. Humans are endowed with the gift of speech for the purpose of opening up creative possibilities. It is a gift that has allowed, or perhaps encouraged, us to evolve quickly, to build relationships, families, and communities.

Unfortunately, many men (and women) have lost the ability to creatively engage in small talk, which, in turn, leads to a singular inability to communicate intimately. Why? Because instead of learning how to use talk to take some creative chances with language, or to consider ideas we haven't considered before, or to move two people from boring, practiced monologues to genuine heartfelt dialogue, we find it is easier to engage in what communication scholars term "phatic communion." Here is an example:

"So how was your day?"

"Fine." Pause. "Yours?"

"Not too bad." Pause. "Anything new?"

"No." Longer pause. "With you?"

"Not really." Longer pause. "So what's for dinner?"

"Oh, I dunno. What do you feel like?"

Very long pause. "We could order pizza."

"Yeah, we could . . . ."

And so on. If your everyday communication with an intimate other tends to resemble the above pattern, chances are good that you think your life is pretty boring. Probably your relationship is pretty stale, as well. It's there, it's with you everyday, and it's comfortably predictable. It's the sandwich you've learned how to rely on, but it's not a meal. It is definitely not very satisfying. And, ultimately, it's not healthy. Research has shown that people who rely on phatic communion as the substance of their relational communication are both less satisfied with those relationships and less able to do much about it. Why? Because talk is the daily bread that sustains and satisfies our desire to be in a relationship. Talk is also a *skilled* activity, and it requires daily practice to improve the level at which it is played.

Sandwiches for Two

When was the last time you really spoke from the heart to each other? When was the last time you really showed each other how much you care? When was the last time you *really* made love?

The good news is you can learn to improve your everyday exchanges of talk, and with it, the quality of your intimate relationships and overall life. Communication is part skill and part art, much like making a sandwich. You can learn how to make better talk simply by bringing in fresh ingredients, or by adding a little basil to what is otherwise just plain mayonnaise.

The idea is to use your imagination to think differently about what a sandwich, or a conversation, can be *about*, or can be *for*. Are you really satisfied with just going through the motions of making small talk, or do you want to use your time together to really explore a topic, an idea, your relationship, your future? Weekends are excellent times for exploring and sharing such talk, which is to say for making something special out of what otherwise will be just another bite of the same old sandwich white.

> A sandwich is all about what you put between the bread; a conversation is all about what you do between "good morning," and "goodnight." In both cases, you have to be able to imagine a better world—a better relationship, a better sandwich—before you can make it.

All change in relationships begins in talk. Adding new ingredients is always an experiment, and maybe a little bit risky. But do you really want to live with "the same old same old?" Are you willing to experiment? To take a chance? To evolve?

Think about that for awhile, while you are learning to make one of my sandwiches. Think about what it is that you *talk about* with your partner. What kind of relationship gets made out of such talk? Do you share your experiences, or just engage in small talk? What kind of talk would you really *like* to share? How can you begin to make that happen?

How's that sandwich of yours shaping up, fella?

LOVE AMONG THE GREENS

"I never saw Susan without feeling a small but

discernible thrill. The thrill was mixed with a feeling of

gratitude that she was with me, and a feeling of pride

that she was with me, and a feeling of arrogance that

she was fortunate enough to be with me. But mostly it

was just a quick pulse along the ganglia which, if it were

audible, would sound a little like woof."

—Robert B. Parker, <u>Paper Doll</u>

A Salad is a Garden of Earthly Delights

A lot of men I have known would rather suffer serious lower intestinal track problems than learn how to prepare a salad, much less make dining on one a natural part of their enjoyment of the culinary life. This, however, will never do. Salads represent one of the essential ways in which men can express individual creativity in the kitchen. Women tend to be very impressed by a well-made one. And besides, guys, they are *good for you*.

None of this matters, though. The important thing to know about salad is that this is one of those things that separate, from a woman's perspective, men who *can* from men who won't *ever* even get a chance to.

Do I have your full attention? Good.

Let's begin by understanding what I *don't* mean by "a salad." First, a salad *isn't* made out of iceberg lettuce, period. Second, this isn't the British Isles, so a "salad" isn't one dubious green leaf beneath yet another helping of potatoes. Third, a salad is not anything left in your refrigerator that can be heaped upon a plate and covered in Thousand Island Dressing.

You can make a very simple salad with a very simple dressing (see Very Simple Salad and Very Simple Dressing, below) or you can elect to create an earthly garden of delight (see Sandra's Signature Salad and Dr. Bud's Balsamic Dressing, further below). Or you can learn to create your own salads that fit somewhere in between these two extremes.

What I am about to pass on to you is a metaphor that transcends the making of salads. It is an *attitude* about salads, what they represent in the world, what they should present and represent between you and the intended she, as a first course, as a first kiss.

A Very Simple Salad

Let's begin with the basics. Here is a tried and true recipe for a Very Simple Salad and two Very Simple Dressings. Imagine it, first of all, as innocence. As the reduction of all that is beautiful in a salad, or in a woman, to its bare delectable essentials.

Raw Materials

1 head of Romaine lettuce (outer leaves removed and discarded; use smaller, inner leaves only)

½ loaf of day-old French (or Seven Grain, or Pumpernickel, or Rye) bread, cut into crouton-sized nuggets

2 Tablespoons olive oil

Freshly slivered Parmesan cheese

Dr. Bud's Mock Caesar Dressing (below)

Tools

Salad spinner (optional, but use it if you have it)

knife

salad bowl

The Blueprint

1. Wash and dry the Romaine leaves.

2. Slice the Romaine leaves horizontally into very thin strips, then half the strips; then half them again.

3. Arrange the leaves on a flat plate.

4. Add croutons (see below for recipe) atop the leaves.

5. Sprinkle some of the slivered Parmesan cheese over the whole thing. Add dressing and serve.

On Croutons

Croutons add a tasty dimension to any salad or soup. Avoid buying the packaged varieties because they are ridiculously expensive and usually taste like overly seasoned cardboard.

To make your own croutons:

1. Cut good leftover bread cut into largish ½" squares.

2. Toss with a little (about ¼ cup per ¼ lb of bread) olive oil. You can add a little fresh pressed garlic to the oil, but this should depend on how well you know the person you are dining with.

3. Roast on a flat baking sheet in a 350 degree oven for 20-30 minutes.

4. Let dry on paper towels until you are ready to toss the salad.

Dr. Bud's Mock Caesar Salad Dressing

This dressing is the perfect accompaniment to the salad above.

Raw Material

1 ½ tablespoons fresh lemon juice

3 Tablespoons extra virgin olive oil

1 large clove of garlic (peeled and pressed)

1 teaspoon coarsely ground black pepper

2 drops of Soy Sauce

Tools

A cruet or other mixing/serving container

The Blueprint

1. Pour all of the ingredients into a tightly sealed container.

2. Shake, rattle, and roll.

3. Pour over the salad *at the table*, toss liberally.

Cheater's Italian Dressing

Some men are just not comfortable mixing seasonings and spices for a salad dressing. I don't know why. Perhaps they don't have the proper ingredients on hand. Perhaps they are pressed for time. Or perhaps they aren't exactly sure what the dressing should ideally taste like. Whatever it is, there is a male reason for the reticence and it is real to these men. I've learned to tolerate (if not fully respect) this, even though I don't entirely understand it. For these men, I offer the following "Cheater's Italian Dressing," which is undeniably delicious and ridiculously easy to make. Like this:

Raw Materials

1 package of dry Good Seasons Italian Salad Dressing

5 Tablespoons extra virgin olive oil

2 Tablespoons balsamic vinegar

A cruet or other mixing/serving container

The Blueprint

1. Pour the vinegar into a dressing container suitable for shaking. If you buy three of the Good Seasons Italian dressings in kit form, you generally get a free salad dressing shaker with it. It's the glass thing with the plastic cover. Use it.

2. Add the Good Seasons mix.

3. Cover the container.

4. Shake for about 10-15 seconds, or until the mixture seems, well, *mixed.*

5. Add the oil and shake again until a thick and richly colored consistency is reached.

On Tossing a Salad

This is a simple but often forgotten step, even in better restaurants. If you don't toss the salad before serving you end up with bites of dry lettuce, followed by bites sopped with dressing. Neither of which is very appealing.

To properly toss a salad:

1. Place the salad items in a large wooden bowl.

2. Add the dressing.

3. Using utensils designed for the purpose—long handled spoon and matching long handled fork—toss gently but with supreme confidence by tossing the greens and every few tosses, rotating the bowl. Do this until the salad leaves appear lightly coated with the salad dressing.

Love Among the Greens

Once tossed, offer to place the salad on the fair maiden's plate by saying something like "May I serve you, dear?" Make a show of it; use a British accent. Women occasionally love their men to act theatrical and silly. If *you* serve the salad, be sure that each plate includes both leaves and croutons.

From my lovely wife's point of view, a salad is a garden of earthly delights. Its natural spontaneous wonder of color, shapes, and textures are of the sort that she might happen upon while strolling down a quiet country lane, or turning suddenly onto an otherwise well-known corner on some imagined uncle's farm.

From my perspective, an advanced salad is more like a naturally beautiful woman. A well-made salad captures and holds your immediate attention. It pleases the eye as much as the palate. This sensuous thing of beauty suggests by its very presence in this moment of your life, that it be *eaten*. Let its essential beauty kiss your mouth, play with your tongue, and so forth.

Where she and I agree then, is on the fact that a salad is not something to be taken lightly. Nor is it something to be tolerated only when smothered with some creamy or soybean-oily crap that pours like some colorful toxic waste from a cheap plastic bottle. Nor do carrots and onions have to be on a salad to made it complete.

A salad, guys, is its own Real Thing. She is Nature. She is Beauty. Respect her, and the world will become a much finer place. Certainly your approach to dinner will be.

Here are our respective approaches to advanced salads. Both are delicious; each one has its own sense of mystery.

Sandra's Signature Salad

One of the best ways to discover what women really want is to watch them. What do they do, for themselves, when nobody else is around? How do they accomplish it? When does what they are doing make them smile?

Armed with these questions I watched my own wife prepare the following salad. And then I watched her do it again. And again. I am not so much a slow learner as a skilled and appreciative observer of womanly actions. As I said, what women do for themselves, repeatedly, is worth watching. And learning from.

Raw Materials

1 head of Boston Bibb Lettuce (washed and spun dry)

1 11-ounce can of mandarin orange segments (drained) or a fresh tangerine

1 13.75-ounce can of quartered artichoke hearts (drained)

1 ripe avocado (peeled, pitted, and sliced)

1 palmful of pecans

Tools

Salad spinner (optional, but use it if you have it)

knife

salad bowl

The Blueprint

1. Tear the lettuce into leaves and then in half.

2. Arrange the lettuce on two plates.

3. Tastefully lump half of the mandarin orange segments (or tangerine) in the center of each plate.

4. Fan the avocado slices clockwise around the plates at 2, 4, 8, and 10 o'clock positions.

5. Arrange the quartered artichokes onto one side of each plate.

6. Cast a few pecans over on the other side.

7. Drizzle Dr. Bud's Raspberry Vinaigrette (see below) over each salad right before serving.

Dr. Bud's BIG Signature Salad

I didn't know this was my "signature salad" until my mother-in-law, Martha Bray, began serving it to her friends under that label. I just thought I was "making a BIG salad," enough for a meal, that always seemed to attract positive reactions from guests. Upon reflection, however, this assembly of garden wonders is an expression of my deep belief in the values of feminine diversity. The essence of which—in each case—is always a good and thorough toss, wherein each mouthful bursts with flavor, with color, and with its very own and very complete *jouissance*.

Raw Materials

1 head of Boston Bibb lettuce (washed, spun dry; each leaf halved)

1 head of red leaf lettuce (washed, spun dry, and torn into bite size pieces)

1 head of Romaine lettuce (washed, spun dry, and thinly sliced)

OR 1 lb of Mesclun mix (mixed baby greens, washed and spun dry)

1 11-ounce can of whole Mandarin orange segments (drained)

1 13.75-ounce can of quartered artichoke hearts (drained)

1 large palmful of toasted and salted sunflower seeds

10-12 Kalamata black olives (cured in olive oil)

3 or 4 firm white or Cremini mushrooms (thinly sliced)

1 ripe tomato (cut into quarters, then cut into quarters again)

1 ripe cucumber (sliced and quartered)

1 stalk celery (thinly sliced)

4 or 6 thin rings of sliced red onion

1 palmful of capers

1 carrot, either julienned or grated (optional)

4 ounces of crumbled feta, bleu, or diced sharp cheddar cheese (optional)

Dr. Bud's Manly Balsamic Vinaigrette or Cheater's Italian Dressing or fresh squeezed orange and/or lemon juice and freshly ground black pepper

Love Among the Greens

Tools

salad spinner

knifes

cutting board

salad bowl

The Blueprint

1. Place the lettuces in a large serving bowl (I prefer a wooden one reserved only for salads).

2. Add the remaining ingredients in any order but reserve the tomatoes, (optional) cheeses, and toasted sunflower seeds for last.

3. At the table when you are ready to serve, pour the whole container of vinaigrette over the salad, and toss gently but thoroughly, or until the leaves just glisten and you can't stand it anymore. *Never add the dressing until you are at the table.* Eat immediately and with great relish.

Serve with warm crusty French bread. You know, those loaves they label "baguettes" in the store? Yeah, them. And by "warm" I mean heat in a 325-degree oven for 3-5 minutes. Butter can be a good idea. Better: butter that has been slightly softened (leave 1 stick of it out on the countertop on a small flat dish while you prepare the salad) and flavored with (a) 1 clove of crushed garlic, or (2) 1 teaspoon of honey and some crumbled walnuts, or (3) a palmful of fresh chopped parsley. Or my own personal favorite, slice the bread into ½" pieces and bathe each piece in extra virgin olive oil into which you have diced or garlic-pressed 1 or 2 garlic cloves.

A Tale of Three Basic Vinaigrettes

One of the reasons I dislike most bottled dressings is because it is so easy to prepare your own vinaigrette at home. Here are three basic recipes to get you started. Master them, and you will develop options of your own.

Dr. Bud's Manly Balsamic Vinaigrette

1 Tablespoon aged black or white balsamic vinegar

2 ½ Tablespoons extra virgin olive oil

1 large clove garlic (peeled and pressed)

¼ teaspoon coarse-ground black pepper

¼ teaspoon red pepper flakes (optional)

1 teaspoon of finely chopped white onion (preferably Vidalia)

Assemble all ingredients and whisk, stir, shake, or otherwise dance the mixture into a thicker, fully aromatic state of being.

Dr. Bud's Gentle Raspberry Vinaigrette

(especially good with Sandra's Signature Salad)

1 Tablespoon raspberry vinegar

2 ½ Tablespoons olive oil

Combine, stir or shake, and drizzle onto the salad.

Old Recipe Italian Vinaigrette

2 Tablespoons red wine vinegar

6 Tablespoons extra virgin olive oil

1 Tablespoon finely diced red onion

1 or 2 large cloves garlic (peeled and finely diced or pressed)

1 teaspoon dried basil

½ teaspoon dried oregano

½ teaspoon dried parsley

½ teaspoon red pepper flakes (optional)

Assemble all the ingredients while performing opera (optional). Stir, shake, or otherwise combine until a thick, rich consistency is reached. May be stored in refrigerator for up to three days (after which the garlic more or less takes control).

Now that you have mastered the basics...

Only your imagination and locally available ingredients limit your salad options. You can experiment with different types of lettuce (again, though, NEVER iceberg!)—red leaf, green leaf, or the newer baby greens sold in supermarkets these days as "mesclun"—or spinach. You can add veggies as the seasons dictate. You can create new dressings.

Really, the world is your salad. Make it up as you go along! Just in case here are a few possibilities to keep you heading in the right direction.

Red Leaf Lettuce Salad with a Blue Cheese Vinaigrette

Use ripe tomatoes, sliced white or cremini mushrooms, sliced and quartered cukes, and a sliced red onion. Follow the recipe for Dr. Bud's Balsamic Vinaigrette, but substitute white wine vinegar for the balsamic; add two tablespoons of crumbled bleu cheese; shake lightly.

Green Leaf Lettuce Salad with Dijon Vinaigrette

Red onion slices, sliced white mushrooms, green olives, strips of sliced red pepper, thinly sliced carrot, grated sharp cheese. Follow recipe for Dr. Bud's Balsamic Vinaigrette, but substitute red wine vinegar for balsamic; add 1 tablespoon of Dijon-style mustard. Shake or stir to desired consistency.

Spinach Salad with Soy Mustard Vinaigrette

Spinach tends to be really dirty so before serving, you need to wash it throughly, tear up the leaves, and tear off the thick stems at the bottoms. Add red onion slices, white mushrooms, croutons, crumbled pecans, crumbled bacon. Some people add slices of hard-boiled eggs to this salad; others crumble feta cheese; some protein-and-cholesterol hounds add both eggs and cheese. For the dressing, mix 6 tablespoons extra virgin olive oil; 1-tablespoon fresh lemon juice; 1-tablespoon soy sauce; 2 teaspoons Dijon mustard; sea salt and black pepper to taste. Assemble all ingredients and shake well.

Mesclun Mix with Dr. Bud's Manly Balsamic Vinaigrette or Old Recipe Italian Vinaigrette

Add thin slices of red onion to 1 pound of Mesclun mix.

Good Listening and Green Leaves

One of the constant complaints women have about men is that we don't listen to them. Research tends to confirm this belief. Fact is, men don't listen well because we don't seem to comprehend that listening is vital to building rapport in an intimate relationship. We think that all that is necessary is for us to do what we are told to do. Sort of like good dogs. So we listen for commands, not questions. We listen for instructions, not emotional tones.

Guys, we can't go on like this. Listening to women communicates two things. First, we are taking them, and what they say, seriously. This is obviously very important to them because it shows *respect* and *concern*. Think about it. You wouldn't get involved intimately with someone who didn't show respect and concern for *you*, would you? Well, being a dog, maybe you would. But you know you shouldn't. And if you even had to *think* about what might be the right answer here, you are a *very* bad dog.

Second, when we listen to women we aren't behaving like most of the rest of the men they have known. This is critical to our relationship because it induces them to respect us. Trust me: most men, in their experience, aren't getting that. And you need to get that before you can get anything else of real value.

Listening, like assembling a fine salad, is really a way of focusing attention on *how the individual parts relate to the whole*. When you listen to a woman, and I mean *really* listen to her, you need to see how what she says relates to what she has been saying all along. For women, *everything is connected*. This is not always true for men. Again, like dogs, we tend to live in and for the moment. Women take a longer view. A much longer view. When a woman looks at you she sees her past and imagines her future. When we look at a woman, well, we *look* at her. See what I mean?

These are differences that matter. A lot. You need to respect this.

Here is a research update for all you guys who think you already have your listening act together. These days it is not advisable to try to prove what a sensitive and self-help literate guy you are by engaging in what is called "active listening." Active listening is where you try to (a) own your own interpretation of what she has been telling you by (b) mirroring back to your partner exactly what she just said; as in "So, what I hear you saying is (fill in the blank with exactly what she just said)." This may have worked during the 70s, when a lot of people smoked pot and couldn't keep things straight for very long, but these days it sounds too cliched and usually only results in the woman believing that she is speaking to a fool. You don't need to mirror back, you just need to pay attention to what she is telling you.

I recommend a lesson in listening based on what I have taught you about making a salad. All salads begin with a goal—to assemble a garden of earthly delights. To listen to your partner, you also need to begin with a goal— to better understand her, to show respect for her experiences—and then consider how you might attain it over dinner.

To attain your goal with a salad requires seeing the relationship of the parts to the whole. To attain your goal for listening requires focusing attention on what she says, connecting the individual ingredients to an overall sense of what she has been saying all along, and being able to ask meaningful questions. By "meaningful," I am especially encouraging you to ask questions about how she feels about what she is saying. Feelings are very important to women. And come on, guys, you know they are important to us, too. We just don't like to talk about them. Women *do*. This is another very important difference, and one that you must learn to respect and adapt to.

My friends, learn to listen well to a woman and you will gain entrance to a very special garden of earthly delights. Love is always best just *beyond* the greens.

Cheers!

PASTA LA VISTA

"She seemed to spend more time

watching me eat than eating herself . . ."

—Max Allan Collins, <u>Carnal Hours</u>

The Poetics of Pasta

This chapter is dedicated to the Poetic of Pasta. It is "poetic" because good pasta, like good poetry, enlivens the senses and delights the soul. It is imagined, created, shaped, poured over, smelled, seen, twirled, tasted, and enjoyed. Again and again and again. Each time, it is newly fulfilling. As natural as the movements of the oceans, the warmth of the sun, and the ineffable wonder of the stars, the enjoyment of pasta completes an ages-old cycle of desire that begins, always, with an arousal of our senses. For this reason, pasta and pasta talk must be driven by vision; together they make a mysterious, poetic statement that, upon its finely articulated and richly melodic breath, moves you and your partner to find the one true shared meaning that lies at the very heart of all human dialogue.

That's the way of its poetry.

However, there is also a very practical side to the pragmatic whys and hows of preparing pasta. Before we wax poetic again, let us turn our attention to it.

Pasta and Passion

Pasta represents one of the four basic food groups for American cuisine: steak (including burgers), chicken, salads, and pasta. Ironically, there are few mainstream (re: affordable) restaurants that can match a pasta made at home. Most of what passes for pasta in institutional places is overcooked durum semolina, burdened with a sugary red sauce—or "doctored" with too much red pepper, garlic, and oregano—and is served by someone who sincerely hopes that by offering to sprinkle some "freshly grated" Parmesan cheese over the top, a "great" tip—er, meal—will be created.

Plu-eeze! Somebody he'p me.

It is like lookin' for love in all the wrong places.

Pasta La Vista

Pasta communicates *passion*. It is a relatively simple fare that carries with it the legendary Italian flare for before, during, and after-dinner romance. Served properly, with ambiance established by a single red rose in a vase on a table for two, accompanied by wine, perhaps a little opera way down low . . . well, what are we here for, anyway, huh? The serving of pasta at the table immediately arouses the nose, sets the mouth to watering, forces the slowly parted lips to pucker. The first taste is pure and sweet, the spices linger on the tongue; the teeth meet pleasant resistance in the *al dente* noodles, but the resistance is short-lived and the experience curiously enticing; and soon, very soon, the tasty object of desire that was, only a moment ago, just an appeal to the senses becomes one with your body. Yes!

We're talkin' *pasta*, pasta la vista, here.

Pasta, at its most basic level, is really about the attraction of seeming opposites. There is the noodle; here is the sauce. Left to itself, the noodle is a shapely, but relatively unappealing fare, and sauces lack a certain something capable of bringing out their best qualities. Bring them together, however, and they seem destined for each other.

However simple this basic recipe for tonguely delight seems, many men mess it up in gender-specific ways. Some of us believe the sauce is *everything*, and the spicier the sauce, the better. This imbalance disturbs the natural harmony that is called for. Some of us believe that if we just heap a pile of sauce over a few overcooked noodles, maybe serve some bread with it, this will do. Unfortunately, this rude approach to what ought to be a subtle and nuanced presentation of self to Other, only suggests our desire to over-control (and a willingness to cover-up) a situation where clearly an honest balance of influences makes for a far more tempting dish.

Guys, let me help you understand the essential connection of pasta and symbolic inducement. What is symbolically communicated by the preparation and presentation of the dish is far more telling about your character, and your love-making proclivities, than you think. With a few easy to learn recipes, you can improve your ability to understand what a woman sees in what and how you eat, and, if necessary, turn this around.

Consider the excellent marinara sauce (see The Essence of Marinara) that begins this section. I place it first because it is very easy to learn how to make, always tastes great, and overall provides a primer on saucing technique to inform all the variations that follow this particular theme.

Next I teach you how to make a rich meat sauce, the old-fashioned American way. If she likes meat-based sauces, this is the one for her. I promise it won't taste like anything you've ever sampled in any chain restaurant, and the raves for it will make you the culinary envy of your pasta peers. Why am I so confident? Simple. The basic recipe comes straight from old Roma, via my Mother's personal cook, Alfoncino, and probably dates back to sometime in the 15th century. Modified for the American palate (i.e., more sauce and meat than any self-respecting Italian would endure), it provides a hearty and satisfying meal. If this sauce is tempting, but you long for a lower-fat version, I've included an alternative.

I also like to experiment with various non-tomato based sauces. My wife's two favorites are reprinted here (Pasta with Green Olives; Pasta with Lemon and Lime Shrimp). I follow these with the pasta recipe that got me started on this book, Pasta with Artichokes, Pecans, and Sundried Tomatoes.

Finally, I include a recipe for a special summer salad nicoise and a winter favorite—stuffed seashells.

The Essence of Marinara

This recipe is derived from a cooking school original by the legendary American chef, James Beard. It is a metaphor for how fundamental ingredients can be married for balance, for harmony, for order. I learned to prepare it from one of his proteges while employed as an apprentice saucier at *The Old South Mountain Inn* in Maryland. The key to success with this recipe lies in being able to slowly cook the tomatoes down to an appropriate thickness, which takes time. You can speed up the process by increasing the heat, but usually at the expense of the flavor. Allow at least two hours to prepare this sauce.

Traditionalists will want to use only fresh Roma tomatoes. This is fine when they are ripe and available, but where I live this is not as often as I like. For this reason I have found that you can gain really good results with good ol' 15-ounce cans of store-bought diced tomatoes. Traditionalists will not accept this, but maybe you will; I do.

Raw Materials

3 lbs of ripe Roma tomatoes (washed and diced) or 4 15-ounce cans of diced red tomatoes (which I always keep on hand for those crunch times)

1 stick of unsalted butter

2 Tablespoons dried basil

(optional) 1 or 2 cloves garlic (peeled and finely chopped)

1 lb angel hair, vermicelli, or other thin pasta

Tools

spaghetti pot with drainer or a large pot

saucepan

cooking screen

large serving bowl

The Blueprint

1. Melt the butter (do NOT use margarine!) over medium heat in a large saucepan.

2. Add tomatoes and stir well.

3. Add the basil and stir again.

4. Reduce heat to a low simmer; cover with a cooking screen to prevent making a royal mess of your stovetop.

5. Stir and taste occasionally, but avoid adding additional basil until the very end.

The sauce will be ready in two hours. If it isn't ready and you MUST EAT RIGHT NOW, then stir in a little (e.g., 1/4-1/2 can) tomato paste. Add another teaspoon or so of fresh basil at the very end of the cooking process.

Serve over any pasta. My favorite for this delicate sauce is angel hair, but any long and thin variety (such as vermicelli) will do nicely. Accompany with a warm loaf of Italian or French bread and butter. Serve with red wine, preferably a good quality Chianti or fruity Beaujolais.

On Choosing Pasta

The good news is you don't need to "roll your own." A study done a couple of years ago compared freshly made pasta with quality store-bought dried varieties and found that (a) there is very little, if any, difference nutrition-ally, and (b) most people are, in fact, better served with the store-bought variety. In terms of taste, I actually prefer dried, if it is a good imported brand such as DeCecco or Colvita. This doesn't mean you shouldn't use fresh dough; it just means you don't have to be embarrassed not to.

Choosing pasta depends on what sauce you plan to offer with it. The thinner the sauce, the thinner your pasta should be. For a basic Marinara, try vermicelli or angel hair. For heartier sauces (anything with meat or shellfish), select a linguine, fettuccine, or regular spaghetti, or try penne, bowties, or ziti.

On Cooking Pasta

Many otherwise intelligent men I know think the key to boiling water for pasta is to bring any old large pot of cold water to a boil over high heat. This is only part of the story. The other parts of the story involve using the proper pot and adding salt and/or olive oil to the brew. First, the pot.

When cooking pasta, you need to use a pot designed for the purpose. By this I mean one of those nice stainless steel units with the lift-out strainer. You can find one in any cook's store and most department stores for under $30. When you buy it, don't use it for anything else. Keep it pure.

The remaining trick to boiling water for pasta involves adding salt and/or olive oil. Wait until a rolling boil occurs, then add 1 tablespoon of sea salt. If you are cooking any of the shaped pastas—bowties, sea shells, ziti, or penne—add 2 tablespoons of olive oil and stir until the large oil slicks turn into many smaller ones. Why add oil? Because it keeps the pasta from sticking together, and from sticking to the pot. After completing these steps, you are ready to add the pasta.

1. Bring a large pot of water to boil over high heat.

2. When a furious, rolling boil has been achieved, add one table-spoon of sea salt and stir.

3. Add the pasta.

4. Cover and bring back to a boil.

5. Uncover and stir the pasta, making sure to gently press the ends of it into the water.

6. Set the timer on your stove for the recommended cooking time on the box of pasta.

Pasta—like shrimp—is cooked before you think it is. If you follow package instructions, you will be very close to that point because most pasta manufacturers purposefully underestimate the cooking times required, knowing, as I'm sure they do, that most Americans overcook pastas. The easiest way to know for sure if the pasta is done is when you can remove a strand from the boiling water and either (a) toss it against an available wall—if it sticks, it's done; or (b) just taste it. It should be slightly resistant to the bite, but not hard. And remember, the pasta will continue to cook after you turn off the heat, drain it, and place it into a serving dish. For this reason, it is always better to undercook it rather than overcook it.

True Meat Sauce: The Old Fashioned American Way

You need to avoid breakfast and lunch, or at least eat lightly, if you plan to prepare this dish for a romantic dinner. Not only is it rich and filling, but chances are good you will not be able to resist tasting it in ever-increasing proportions as the sauce thickens and the flavors meld. Trust me on this. One word of caution: while it is worth every mouthful, this sauce takes 4 hours to prepare and cook.

Raw Materials

1 lb of coarsely ground chuck or sirloin

1 lb of coarsely ground pork

2 large red onions (one peeled and chopped; the other peeled but left whole)

3 or 4 cloves of garlic (peeled and coarsely chopped)

1 Tablespoon sea salt

1 teaspoon black Java pepper

4 15-ounce cans diced tomatoes and juice (do not drain)

1 cup red wine (good quality Burgundy or Beaujolais)

1 Tablespoon dried basil

½ Tablespoon dried oregano

½ Tablespoon dried parsley (if you use fresh, make it ½ cup)

2 bay leaves

8-10 whole cloves (NOT garlic; whole cloves, as in the kind your granny used in ham)

1 green pepper (washed and chopped)

1 red pepper (washed and chopped)

1 carrot (grated)

1 lb of hearty pasta, such as spaghetti, fettuccini, or penne

Tools

large cooking pot

spaghetti pot or large pot to cook the spaghetti

knife

cutting board

grater

The Blueprint

1. Begin by browning the meats over medium-high heat in a large pot.

2. After the meat is throughly browned, drain the grease from the pot.

3. Add the garlic and the chopped red onion to the meat; stir several times. Allow the onions to become translucent (i.e., they aren't white anymore, and you can almost see through them), and continue to cook on medium for about three minutes.

4. Add the salt, pepper, and 4 cans of diced tomatoes. Stir several times.

5. Add the wine, basil, oregano, parsley, and bay leaves. Stir again.

6. While you are waiting for this mixture to return to a simmer, push the whole cloves into the remaining onion (I generally use 4 per side and 3-4 in the middle).

7. When the sauce is simmering, place the onion directly into the center of the sauce.

8. Cover, reduce the heat to low, stir and sample occasionally over the next two or three hours.

9. When you think the sauce is just about ready, add the green and red peppers and the grated carrot. Stir thoroughly, do NOT put the lid back on the pot, and cook for another 20-30 minutes, or until the recent additions are tender.

10. Taste for seasonings; add a pinch of additional basil and oregano if necessary. If the sauce gets too thick, add some (1/4-1/2 cup) more wine.

This rich sauce must be served over pasta thick enough to handle the weight. I recommend fettuccine or regular spaghetti (if you prefer long pastas) or penne. Offer some freshly grated Parmesan cheese, if you like. A hearty Burgundy or Pinot Noir wine should be selected.

On Peeling Garlic

The smell of fresh garlic on fingers appeals less to women than to dogs. For this reason, either wear plastic gloves when peeling garlic, or use either one of my simpler methods, both of which are decidedly more manly:

Method 1: Place the clove on a cutting board and smash it with the handle of a paring knife. The skin will fall away easily.

Method 2: Purchase one of the commercially-available green plastic tubes manufactured for this purpose. Place one clove of garlic at a time inside the tube and roll once aggressively. You will hear the satisfying snap and crackle of skin falling away from the clove. Remove the garlic and dispose of the skin.

The Lower-Fat Rich Meat Sauce Alternative

Use 98% fat-free ground turkey breast instead of the ground chuck and pork. This version makes a tasty sauce, but the meat will remain white, which somewhat detracts from the overall appearance. If this troubles you, try substituting a green spinach or black squid pasta. The breast meat will still be white, but the colorful mix will enhance the overall presentation.

Pasta with Olives

My wife *loves* pasta, and she loves green olives. I created this dish to satisfy her craving for both of them. If you and your date/spouse/partner/ significant Other are pasta and olive lovers, it will satisfy you, too.

Raw Materials

2 Tablespoons extra virgin olive oil

1 clove garlic (peeled and finely chopped)

1 7-ounce jar of pitted green olives (yes, you can use the big Spanish Queen ones stuffed with pimento, if you like)

1 lb linguine

1 15-ounce can 99% fat-free chicken broth

Tools

large cooking pot

spaghetti pot or large pot to cook the spaghetti

The Blueprint

1. Bring the chicken broth to a low simmer over medium heat in a large pot.

2. As you are doing this, cook the linguine for *half of its recommended time* in boiling water.

3. Drain and transfer quickly to the large pot containing the simmering chicken broth.

4. Cook the linguine the remaining time in the broth, or until most of the broth has been absorbed.

5. While you waiting for the linguine to cook, sauté the garlic in the oil (always heat the oil first, then add the garlic),.

6. Add the olives and bring to a warm and fragrant overall presence.

Toss in a large serving dish with the linguine and any leftover chicken broth. Offer some freshly grated Parmesan cheese. Serve with a nice subtle white wine—Sauvignon Blanc or Pinot Grigio, for example—of your choice.

Pasta with Lemon and Lime Shrimp

This is an excellent summertime dish. Accompanied with a simple green salad and some crusty French bread, it is all pleasure.

Raw Materials

1 lb large Gulf shrimp (peeled and de-veined)

Juice of 1 large lemon

Juice of 1 large lime

1 clove garlic

2 Tablespoons extra virgin olive oil

½ cup dry white wine or vermouth

1 red pepper (thinly sliced)

Coarsely ground black pepper to taste

1 lb linguine or fettucine

Tools

skillet

spaghetti pot or large pot to cook the spaghetti

2 bowls

knife

cutting board

The Blueprint

1. Bring water to boil for the pasta.

2. Place equal amounts of the shrimp in two non-corrosive bowls.

3. Squeeze the lemon over the shrimp in one bowl, the lime over the other.

4. Stir and allow to marinate for five or ten minutes.

5. Prepare the pasta in the boiling water according to package instructions.

6. While the pasta is cooking, heat the oil in a skillet, add the garlic, and stir for 30 seconds.

7. Add the wine or vermouth and bring to a boil.

8. Add the shrimp (and remaining juices), return to boil.

9. Add the sliced red peppers on top of the shrimp.

10. Cover the skillet and turn off the heat.

In three minutes the shrimp will be cooked. Toss with the drained pasta. Add the pepper to taste. Serve with any of the white wines recommend in the section *On Wine.*

On De-Veining Shrimp

I'm not going to try to explain to you why this is a good idea because if you have to ask, then chances are good you either flunked biology in high school and/or have very poor personal hygiene habits. Or, God forbid, both. Suffice it to say you need to do this, and the shrimp will look more appealing as a result. Just take my word for it. This is something you *must* do.

Peel the shrimp first. Take a small, sharp knife, turn the shrimp so the back-side is facing you, and cut a straight line about 1/16th of an inch deep, ¾'s of the way down the middle. Remove the black stuff, which should come out as a more or less intact unit. Wash you hands when you are done.

Pasta with Artichokes, Pecans, and Sundried Tomatoes

This is the dish I wrote about in the *Preface*, the one that got me started writing this cookbook. It is a Dr. Bud signature dish and can be prepared in less than 30 minutes. Try it, you'll love it.

Raw Material

1 13.75-ounce can quartered artichokes

½ lb pecan halves

½ - 3/4 of a 7-ounce jar of sundried tomatoes in extra virgin olive oil (slice the tomatoes into very thin strips; use half of the olive oil in the jar for sautéing the artichokes)

1 15-ounce can diced tomatoes (drained)

1 clove garlic (peeled and finely chopped)

¼ teaspoon red pepper flakes

Sea salt and black Java pepper to taste

1 lb penne, rotini, ziti, or other short, stout pasta

Tools

skillet

spaghetti pot or large pot to cook the spaghetti

large serving bowl

Pasta La Vista

The Blueprint

1. Prepare pasta according to package instructions.

2. As you await the pasta, sauté the garlic in the sundried tomato olive oil for 30 seconds; add the remaining ingredients, and stir.

3. When the pasta is done and drained, toss in a large serving bowl with the sauce.

Serve with warmed sourdough rolls and a sturdy red (e.g., Cabernet Sauvignon, Merlot, or Pinot Noir) or white (e.g., White Cabernet, Chardonnay) wine.

Summer Salad Nicoise

Pasta salads are great for hot summer lunches or dinners. This recipe combines the crisp cool textures of leafy lettuces with the appetite-satisfying flavors of either tuna or chicken. In either format, we add black olives, capers, and red tomatoes. We drizzle on a basic vinaigrette. You can add other varieties of summer veggies to this rich mixture as you wish. Enjoy!

Raw Material

1 head of Bibb lettuce

OR 1 large bunch of Mesclun mix

1 can of water-packed all-white meat canned tuna

OR 1/2 lb of freshly grilled tuna

OR 1/2 lb of leftover grilled chicken

1 7-ounce jar of black (Greek) olives in olive oil or brine

2-3 Tablespoons of green capers

1-2 ripe red tomatoes, quartered, then halved

Bow tie pasta

Basic Balsamic Vinaigrette or Raspberry Vinaigrette (see *Love Among the Greens* chapter) or 2½ tablespoons of freshly squeezed orange juice and 1 tablespoon Extra Virgin Olive Oil, mixed

Tools

spaghetti pot or large pot to cook the spaghetti

large oval platter

The Blueprint

1. Prepare the pasta according to the directions on the box.

2. Wash and drain the lettuce leaves, arrange them on a large oval platter.

3. Place a layer of pasta over the lettuce.

4. Add the sliced tuna or chicken chucks according to your own preferences, using some precise mathematical table that only you understand (yeah, right!).

5. Do the same thing with the olives, capers, and tomatoes. When you are ready to serve it at the table, drizzle on either of the vinaigrettes. Serve with sweet iced tea, ice-cold lemonade, or sparkling water. If you are deeply Southern, try Lynchburg Lemonade (recipe available only from Jack Daniel's Distillery, Lynchburg, Tennessee). Or, simply serve with a good quality California white wine or Blush Zinfadel.

Guy-At-Home-Alone Night

Want to cook something for yourself that probably would not be well-received by a woman? The above technique for preparing pasta can be successfully adapted for a guy-at-home-alone night. Here are two variations on a common theme, sure to delight your senses and appeal to your sense of manliness.

Man of the House Garlic 'n' Oil sauce

I have no idea where this recipe came from, but whomever invented it deserves a revered place in the Pasta Hall of Fame. It is sooooo easy to prepare, and can be fully created in less than 10 minutes! Just don't fix this when she's around.

 Raw Materials

2 Tablespoons good quality olive oil

1 15-ounce can 99% fat-free chicken broth

2-5 cloves of garlic, diced

Salt and freshly ground black Java pepper to taste

½ lb of any pasta

Tools

spaghetti pot or large pot to cook the spaghetti

knife

cutting board

man size bowl

The Blueprint

1. Boil the water, add the pasta, stir, and cook for *half of the length of time* suggested on the box.

2. Heat the chicken broth in a large saucepan until just short of boiling.

3. When the pasta is half-way cooked, drain it and add it to the saucepan with the chicken broth.

4. Raise the heat to boiling and continue cooking for the remainder of the time suggested on the box.

5. Saute the garlic in the oil over medium heat for about 30 seconds—don't burn it.

6. Add to the chicken broth. Stir.

7. Add salt and pepper to taste. Place on a dish.

Sit.

Eat.

Smile . . .

Licorice Fish Pasta

This recipe was given to me by my pal Eric Eisenberg. It is a wonderfully-scented and startling appealing concoction, but it is best to make this dish when you can open all the windows and air out the house afterward.

Pasta La Vista

Raw Material

2 Tablespoons good quality olive oil

1 head of fennel; green tops removed, white bottoms thinly sliced

OR 1 Tablespoon dried fennel seeds, thoroughly crushed

1 clove garlic, peeled and diced

1 small jar sardines, packed in olive oil

1 15-ounce can 99% fat-free chicken broth

½ lb of any pasta, but vermicelli works especially well

Tools

spaghetti pot or large pot to cook the spaghetti

knife

cutting board

man size bowl

The Blueprint

1. Heat the chicken broth in a large saucepan.

2. Boil water, add the pasta, cook for half the time suggested.

3. Drain the pasta and transfer to the saucepan with chicken broth.

4. Meanwhile, heat the oil in a large skillet, add the garlic and sardines.

5. When the sardines break up and begin to dissolve, add the fennel.

6. Cook until very fragrant, which won't be very long.

7. Add to the pasta and broth. Stir wildly. Surrender to the fragrance.

Remember to open the windows and air out the house *before* she gets back.

What Men Communicate While They Eat

Women pay attention to everything about us. They notice the little things. They notice the large things. They comment on all things. Mostly, we don't behave this way.

Women develop theories about men based on how—as well as what—we eat. Remember, women connect this thing to that thing, and that thing to everything, and everything, ultimately, to everything else. They process information constantly, comparing present experiences to past ones, to future possibilities. Maybe to future pastabilities, too.

Pardon me, I couldn't resist that pun. My point here is a simple, yet profound one: Nonverbal communication during dinner accents verbal communication to produce rich, finely-detailed interpretations of meaning. Sometimes, the nonverbal element is even more revealing, indicating to women what we *really* mean, or are thinking about. Dangerous stuff, nonverbal communication.

> From a woman's perspective, our nonverbal communication at dinner conveys both meanings and secrets. So we need to learn to pay closer attention to what it is that we are communicating by the way we eat.

Pasta presents a perfect case study in nonverbal communication. It is a slippery dish, full of opportunities for wild chewing, moaning, grunting, sucking, and even slurping. If you've ever watched your average dog dig into a bowl of leftover pasta, you get the general idea. Similarly, if you watch most men eat pasta you see pretty much the same thing. From a woman's point of view, this is disgusting, fascinating, and ultimately revealing. How we eat is a key to who we *really* are.

Pasta La Vista

I learned to pay attention to this connection when having lunch with a pronounced feminist pal o' mine in Philadelphia. We were attending a communication conference together and, at break-time, I said I was going to South Street to get a real Philly cheesesteak. "Anyone wanna come with me?" Several people did. She was one of them. We found a stand on the street nearby. I ordered mine with sauce and onions, and began chowing down. It was *good. Very* good. Admittedly, I am an enthusiastic eater. Eating a cheesesteak enthusiastically, particularly one dripping with red sauce and slathered with fried onions, often means that I appear less than entirely civilized. So be it. The cheesesteak is usually worthy. This one was.

I noticed that I was being watched. Observed. Analyzed. By *her*. She wore a large, obtrusive smirk. She seemed to be considering something deep and humorous. So between mouthfuls, I managed: "What?" She said: "I like the way you eat. I never trust a man who won't get sloppy in front of me."

Well, it's not at all what I would have predicted from her. I mean, most guys believe that we need to be more guarded about our hound-like qualities, eating being one of them. So this statement stuck with me. Over the years I've checked it out with other women. Turns out that most of them agree with the original line. It has something to do with honesty. With passion. With inherent, genuine, beastliness. Or maybe it is just of being sure enough of yourself to enjoy what you are eating in front of someone else.

There are limits to this, of course. No woman I've ever met enjoyed watching a man chew with his mouth open. This disgusts even me. No woman thinks highly of a man who makes a lot of noises while eating. They hierarchically separate sighs of pleasure and the occasional moan from outright pig-like grunting or boar-like flinging of foodstuffs wildly about in the air.

Yet I have also learned that these connections run much deeper than the obviousness of all that.

Women are consumed by a preoccupation with images. Our culture creates this, and we can blame the media perhaps, but nevertheless it is the case. Women pay a lot of attention to how we look when we do things. And the more savvy the woman, the more likely she will pay more attention to how we eat. How we eat, guys, is an image, an emblem, a sign, of who we really are.

I'm not talking hairstyles. Your hair can be coifed. It is a little more than a lie that lays atop your head. Ditto for clothing. It's important, but it is purchased. Unless you are a complete bozo, matching colors and staying more or less fashionably attired is not that hard. You get points for expensive, well-made materials and for contributing your own individual style to what you wear, but this is only to be expected. Our culture values the buck, and it values the individual. Put one and one together and what do you get? Duh.

Fortunately, good women are deeper than that. They are interested in how the parts contribute to the whole, how what we look like complements, contradicts, or contributes to what we claim to be, or say we want "us" to become.

This communication truth requires further scrutiny. Particularly at dinner.

Women see our mouths as symbolic representations of our overall approach to relationships, and to making love. Do we think about what we are eating while we are doing it, or is our mind elsewhere? This is potentially significant. Are we interested in holding a conversation, or even engaging in dialogue, while we are enjoying a meal together? Or are we completely caught-up in the solo pleasure of chewing—or worse, distracted by sports on teevee? Do we comment on how she is enjoying the meal while we are eating, or after? Hmmm. Think about these things, these small and seemingly natural gestures, my friends.

Pasta La Vista

Nothing is without meaning to a woman. And everything *is* connected.

Our mouths only tell part of our story. Whether it is part of our cultural history or merely an accurate reflection of a deeper meaning, women consider our *eyes* to truly be mirrors of our souls. What we do with them during dinner is all-important. Are we looking at the wonder that is her, or at the diminishing contents of our plates? Do we appear to be reflecting on what she is saying, or are our thoughts elsewhere? Perhaps *with* someone else? Are we at peace in our souls, or is there something disturbing going on, way down there? Do we have that essential balance of fire and gentleness, of raw creativity and civil constraint, that women crave?

Our *hands*, while eating, indicate how seriously we take pleasures of the flesh. I knew an older man, once, a major communication scholar from Iowa, who spoke eloquently with his hands during every conversation. His hands appeared to mold and fashion the words as he spoke, there was art in the curving of his fingers around key themes and phrases. Women inevitably fell in love with him, completely and with some obvious abandon. Younger women, older women, women of all races and national origins, you name it, if she was a woman and she got involved in a conversation with this man, well, that was pretty much that. I never knew if any of them ever acted on their inclinations, nor did I ever ask. In truth, I didn't want to know. I was still a young man. My hands were not yet as articulate.

The overall point here is that hands are sources of *profound* communication to women. Clean them, tend to them, trim your fingernails, but most importantly, allow your hands the freedom to add a new level of sensuous meanings to the how of what you say.

Pasta is food that creates a special space in our lives for genuine sensuous pleasures. To eat pasta with a partner is to enter that space with a fuller appreciation for the rich, complex meanings, tastes, moods, that may be contained there.

Pasta is a metaphor for the richness and complexity of intimate human sharing. Do not be afraid to feed her, or yourself.

Cheers!

SPICING THINGS UP

Pike said, "Are you still thinking about her?"

"Yes."

"Then think about this. You've taken her as far as is right. Wherever she's going, she has to get the rest of the way on her own. That's not only the way it is. That's the way it should be."

—Robert Crais, <u>Voodoo River</u>

Love is Spicy

Love *is* spicy. Experiencing it creates a profound rupture in the ordinary and everyday business of living. Its arrival punctuates otherwise uneventful moments with joy, creates a strong need to recognize and deal with one's own desires. Its moment makes a shared, yet private space for idle wanting in the velocity rush of life, for the pursuit of timeless pleasure, for unabashed lazy nakedness, for deep and sustained breathing. Its particular presence in our lives heightens and deepens the senses, improves the electrical flow of energy across millions of synapses, makes the heart beat louder and faster, increases the blood flow to biologically predetermined areas. The emerging heat enlarges the immediate need for contact, for primal deep inner penetration, for a whole body and mind experience whose meaning is perfectly clear.

Whew.

Indeed.

Yes, my friend, love is *spicy.* For this reason, I have devoted a special and central place in this cookbook for spicy recipes and for a discussion of spicy talk. For spicy recipes of a Southwestern and/or Tex-Mex origin. And for spicy talk that cuts across all borders, all boundaries, all ways of taking the conversation to the next level.

Portobello Mushroom and Wild Rice Enchiladas with Spicy Black Beans

This dish emerged one afternoon as I was trying to conceive of a low-fat, vegetarian, Tex-Mex combination that would please my wife and myself. Frankly, I had not been very impressed by previous vegetarian Tex-Mex efforts, beyond the myriad of burritos you can make with a decent black bean recipe. My wife, well, she just won't eat beans, period. Says they don't have a pleasing consistency, which baffles me. Personally, I think her resistance is largely due to the obvious bad rep that prepared beans often have. You know what I mean. At any rate, some issues are not worth debating in our household, and this clearly is one of them.

I had recently grilled some portobello mushrooms, red peppers, and zucchini (after marinating this mix for about 10 minutes in garlic and olive oil) as a side dish for a green peppercorn encrusted porterhouse steak (see p. 138-141). It occurred to me that sautéing the same basic combination could produce a whole new enchilada. From that basic leap of faith, it wasn't too much of a stretch to envision an adding wild rice and a basic red salsa with traditional green chilies. Add some of that timesaving, already grated, Mexican Four Cheese blend available on the cheese aisle of any respectable food store, bake until bubbly, and YUM!

From this vision, I eventually came up with the following low-fat (except for the cheeses) menu. If you are a guy who enjoys his Tex-Mex, and if you know someone special who would enjoy it with you, then try this one.

> NOTE: Preparation time for this dish is a factor. Cilantro is a wonderful ingredient, but takes a long time to de-stem and chop. Also, there is a good bit of time invested in chopping, dicing, mixing, and assembling the various parts of this dinner. But the outcome is well worth it! For this reason, I recommend following this precise plan. Allow about two hours to make this dish, an hour of which will be preparation.

The Black Beans

You might question the sanity of someone going to this much trouble for beans, but once you have had them, I promise you will make them again and again and again. Because she will ask for them again and again and again and isn't that the point?

Raw Materials

1 lb dried black beans

2 Tablespoons olive oil

2 medium onions (peeled and chopped)

4 good sized cloves of garlic (peeled and chopped very small)

2 good sized Jalapena peppers (remove seeds and stems)

1 teaspoon cumin powder

1 teaspoon coriander power

1 teaspoon Mexican oregano powder

1 teaspoon sea salt

½ teaspoon black Java pepper

½ bunch of fresh cilantro (rinsed, de-stemmed, and chopped)

2 bay leaves

2 teaspoons dried tarragon

1 12-ounce bottle of good Mexican lager

Two quarts of water

Non-fat sour cream (place a dollop on the beans when you serve them)

Tools

colander

2 large pots

large mixing bowl for assembling salsa

knife

cutting board

The Blueprint

1. Open the one-pound plastic sack of dried black beans.

2. Pour the beans into a colander and rinse very thoroughly (at least two minutes). Keep turning the colander to ensure that all the beans are cleaned. As you turn the colander, be on the lookout for nasty little black or brown stones that often accompany the beans into the sack. The last thing you want to have happen is for her to break a tooth on something that wasn't supposed to be in the dish anyway, right?

3. Place the olive oil in a pot large enough to hold both the beans and the eventual liquids, realizing that beans will expand to about three times their dried size as they cook. I seriously recommend using a heavy nonstick pot, such as Circulon for this task. As the beans cook they absorb the liquids and can stick to other surfaces; when this happens, chances are good you will scrape them from the bottom, at which point they break open and become mushy. To do a better job with beans, use a better pot.

4. Heat the oil on medium high until it moves easily across the pot when the pot is lightly shaken.

5. Add the chopped onion and sauté for two or three minutes, or until the onions are almost translucent.

6. Add the chopped garlic and sauté for another minute or so.

7. Add the beans and stir three or four times.

8. Cover the beans in two quarts of cold water and bring the mixture to a solid boil. Stir two or three times, just for the hell of it.

9. Add one halved Jalapena pepper (with the fiery seeds and stems removed) to the beans and water mix. Cover, reduce heat to a low simmer, and cook for about two hours. By then most of the water will have been absorbed, and you will have de-stemmed and chopped the fresh cilantro and mixed all of the remaining spices in a small bowl.

10. Add one 12-ounce bottle of Dos Equis Special Lager or Corona (don't use Corona Light, or any light beer, for that matter) to the beans. Stir again, enjoy the aroma. Now add the spices you mixed together in the bowl. Stir several times, to ensure an equitable distribution of these resources. Cover and continue cooking for another hour.

The Wild Rice

Wild rice takes a full hour to cook. Beginning it at this point in the process assures that it will be ready for assembly in the enchilada at the right time.

Here is the easiest part of this recipe. Purchase a box of wild rice (you will find it in the rice section of your supermarket). Follow the package instructions, to wit:

1. Rinse the rice in a colander until the water runs clear. Shake the colander to get rid of excessive water build up.

2. Find a suitable pot, recognizing that rice expands as it cooks.

3. Add three cups of water to one cup wild rice. Cover, bring to a boil. Stir.

4. Reduce heat to low simmer, cover again, and cook for 45-60 minutes, or until most of the water is absorbed.

5. Now add a teaspoon of sea salt to it.

On Cilantro

For guys unfamiliar with cilantro, some advice. First rinse the greens well, and then shake dry. Now you have a choice to make. You need to de-stem the leaves, which means your choice is whether to use kitchen shears or your hands. Either way, you need to make sure the leaves are chopped, ripped, or torn to manageable proportions—and the stems discarded—before you add them to the beans. And either way, you can practice your Karioke techniques to a good blues CD while you are doing it. I like Jonny Lang's "Lie to Me," but no doubt you have your own favorites.

The Salsa

The salsa will be used both inside the enchiladas and, in combination with the four cheeses, as a topping. For this recipe I use a basic red salsa, which is mild, a little sweet, and owes its seductive flavor to a blend of lime juice and fresh cilantro more so than to the green chilies and onion in it. In my experience, unless your woman plays rugby, this mild salsa is usually preferred.

Lady's Choice: Mild Red Salsa

4 15-ounce cans of diced red tomatoes (drained)

1 bunch of fresh cilantro (rinsed and chopped)

1 small onion (Vidalia, if possible, peeled and chopped)

1 can of chopped green chilies (drained)

Juice of one good sized lime

1 teaspoon white sugar

1 teaspoon sea salt (or more, if you prefer)

¼ bottle of good Mexican lager (optional)

Assemble all of the ingredients and stir gently until the cilantro is well blended. Cover the bowl and place in the refrigerator for an hour or so to chill. Serve a little of this salsa with tortilla chips as an appetizer.

Double check to see that the fire under the beans is way down low. You are after the sort of simmer that looks, well, *languid,* like something you would expect a really Southern woman's syrupy drawl to sound like, if it were a sight rather than a sound. Any higher temperature than this, and chances are good you will need to add more water or beer (I prefer beer, unless I'm seriously into drinking it) before the beans arrive at their own personal cooked nirvana.

The Enchildas

 Raw Materials

½ lb fresh Portobello mushrooms (wiped clean—NOT rinsed! See *On Mushrooms,* later in this chapter.)

½ lb fresh Crimini mushrooms (wiped clean)

1 medium red pepper (sliced into strips, then diced)

1 medium zucchini (rinsed, sliced, and quartered)

2 Tablespoons olive oil

10 flour tortillas suitable for burrito-sized holdings

1 8-ounce packages (about two cups) of Sargento Mexican Four Cheese mix

About two cups of the mild red salsa

1 8-ounce container of non-fat sour cream

Tools

knife

cutting board

large sauté pan

large skillet

large baking dish

The Blueprint

1. Rub each Portobello lightly with a moist paper towel. Cut each of them it into ¼" slices, then dice those slices. You want each piece of 'shroom to be about the size of a penny. Repeat the same procedure with the Criminis. Set aside.

2. Slice the red pepper into strips, and then dice into penny-sized units. Set aside.

3. Cut the zucchini into ¼" slices, then quarter them. These will re-semble fat nickels. Set aside.

4. Heat the olive oil on medium high in a large sautéing pan.

5. Meanwhile, heat, on medium, a dry pan large enough to hold the tortilla.

6. Begin sautéing the Portobellos and Criminis (because you want the mushrooms to absorb most of the oil); stir them as you deem necessary, but remember the idea here is to heat them, not to burn them.

7. Add in the zucchini and red pepper, stir two or three times, then cut the heat down to low. Don't overcook the veggies!!! Probably this whole procedure should take no longer than three minutes.

8. Toss a tortilla into the dry pan, cook it for about 30 seconds or until it begins to bubble, and flip it over and repeat the same procedure on the other side.

9. Remove from the pan; put on a plate.

10. Toss in a second tortilla.

11. Slap about a tablespoon of non-fat sour cream in the middle of the tortilla, then add in a few veggies and a spoonful of wild rice.

12. Run a thick line of salsa over the whole mess, and add a little cheese (not too much).

13. Wrap the tortilla by folding over the bottom about 1 inch, the top down about an inch, then roll the tortilla across the mixture from the left to the right.

14. Place in a baking dish with the final fold facing down.

15. Grab the second tortilla from the dry pan and flip it over. Probably you will need to reduce the heat to between medium and low at this point, because the skillet will have absorbed enough heat to have systemically increased the resulting temperature.

16. Repeat the same process for filling the enchilada as above, but remember to toss in a new tortilla BEFORE you begin filling the heated one.

17. Do this until you run out of tortillas or veggies. If you make a manly burrito-sized enchilada, this will be sooner than later, so be sure to gauge your proportions accordingly. In my kitchen, I do about seven or eight, and each one is capable of providing a full and satisfying meal sided with the rice and beans.

18. Lightly cover the baking dishes with salsa and cheese.

19. Bake in a 350-degree oven for about twenty minutes, or until the cheese starts to bubble and your stomach begins to shout, "feed me!"

This recipe calls for attention to *timing*. Remember what I said in the introduction about linear versus contextual time? Here is a prime example. In linear time, it really doesn't take very long to sauté the veggies in the oil, heat each tortilla separately, and fill the flour wrapper. But contextually, each part of this process must be accomplished as if it were part of an overall system, which means that you need to heat each tortilla *while* you are preparing the enchiladas. How long it takes you to do one thing will inevitably influence how long it takes you to do the other.

The good news is that not much very bad can happen to your dinner if you screw up. You can always turn off the flame under the veggies and just let them sit there in the pan. You can throw away a burnt tortilla or two. And unless you are completely into trashing countertops, you can actually try to be a little bit careful when filling the tortillas with the veggies, the rice, the salsa, the cheeses, and the sour cream.

So don't worry. Just do the best you can. In the end, the whole dish will be covered with more cheese and salsa, so what the hell?

The beans are done when they are soft and begin to fall apart when stirred. Serve warm with a dollop of sour cream, a small side dish of Mexican Four Cheese mix and some tortilla chips. If you have leftovers, you can add some Sante Fe Red Rice underneath them, freeze the whole thing in one of those plastic containers, and take it for lunch next week. Or you can puree the beans in your Cuisinart and use it as a spicy dip when friends come over.

Carefully remove a tortilla from the baking dish with a large spatula. Place it smack in the middle of the serving plate. Scoop some beans to the right, and some salsa to the left. Garnish with a handsome little cilantro leaf on the tortilla, and a heart-shaped dollop of sour cream on the beans.

At my table we drink Mexican beer with this concoction. San likes Dos Equis or Corona, but I prefer Negra Modelo. Other people we know serve this sort of fare with a good Pinot Blanc or perhaps Red Zinfadel. Drink what you want. The important thing is to enjoy all of it . . . .

On Leftovers

If you are moderately bright citizen, chances are good that you will notice that you have leftovers. Probably you made eight enchiladas, served one to the lady and one for yourself to start, then maybe each of you ordered up seconds. Whatever. My guess you now have four perfectly good enchiladas, all dressed up with no place to go. What to do?

I hate waste. It is bad for the global economy, bad for the ecology of the planet, and a definite sign of a kind of overall, affluent carelessness. Remember that metaphoric scene toward the end of The *Great Gatsby*, where Nick Carroway spies Jay and Daisy sucking the meat off chicken bones after their affluent self-absorption coalesced to produce the death of Jay's girlfriend, Myrtle? Nick's on-target observation is that these are careless people, not evil people, but people who never had to be accountable for their actions.

This scene has never left me. I think of it often when I enter a kitchen and see perfectly good food that requires a second chance. But in image-conscious America, nobody likes to eat "leftovers." Probably it is the negative connotation of the word "leftover," which conjures up images of second-handedness. Perhaps we should learn from the successes of luxury car dealerships, who now advertise "pre-owned" (but re-certified) vehicles and whose sales force is specifically forbidden from ever uttering the world "used."

So what we have here are four pre-cooked enchiladas. And maybe half a pot of perfectly spiced beans. There may even be some leftover—er, excuse me—pre-prepared wild rice, stewing in its own juices. I suggest placing each enchilada in a plastic, freezer-suitable, airtight container (think: Rubbermaid Saver Server), surrounding it with a few beans and some rice, and freezing it for later use as a lunch that will no doubt surprise your co-workers and astonish your friends. You gain the advantage of a tasty meal and the admiration of your colleagues. You save money. And you prove that you are not a careless person.

On Mushrooms

Why should you wipe mushrooms instead of rinsing them? The answer is simple: mushrooms are actually little aliens, who use water to morph into mind-altering, mood-changing substances.

Just kidding.

The real reason is that mushrooms are *sponges*. They absorb water (or wine, or beer, or whatever fluid you offer them). Thus saturated, their otherwise intense and earthy flavor is severely compromised. So, too, will be the flavor in your recipe. Don't do it. Just wet a paper towel and LIGHTLY rub the surface of the 'shroom.

Now that you've mastered the basic skill set ...

Enchiladas are amenable to many enticing combinations. So is rice. In the above recipe, even the beans can be altered to create exciting new possibilities. Here are some of my favorites . . . .

Sour Cream Chicken Enchiladas

Using the same basic format, substitute cooked (as in pulled off the carcass of a baked, roasted, or grilled barnyard fowl) meat for the mushrooms, peppers, zucchini, and wild rice. I like to use long, very thin strips of chicken meat, which I then mix with nonfat sour cream and 1 tablespoon of diced green chilies or scallions. I use 1 cup of chicken meat to ½ cup of sour cream. Omit the salsa on the inside of the enchilada. Some cheese lovers may prefer to add some Mexican Four Cheese mix to the sour cream and chicken combination, but I generally don't.

Feta Cheese and Grilled Shrimp Enchiladas

Substitute large grilled shrimp (I marinate mine in lime juice, black pepper, and cilantro for five minutes prior to grilling; marinate much longer and you have escabeche and you don't really need to cook them) for the chicken and ¼ cup of crumbled Feta cheese for the sour cream. Note: Only buy the feta cheese that comes in little containers with water. Instead of mixing the meat and cheese together, just place three or four shrimp in each enchilada and crumble a little bit of Feta cheese on top. Fold as per usual. Cover with salsa and cheese as per usual. Savor the difference.

Sante Fe Red Rice

Nowadays there is a myriad of flavored and seasoned rice available in most supermarkets. Some brands are delicious, others make you wish you hadn't even considered it. In my experience, Coyote Café and Paul Prudhomme brands are best, particularly if you follow the "Preferred Preparation" instructions on the side of the package. Usually this just means adding olive oil and an onion to the recipe, maybe a can of diced tomatoes. When you are in a hurry and can make do with one of these prepared brands, do so. Hide the box, though.

Spicing Things Up

For Tex-Mex or Southwestern purists, however, there is nothing quite like making your own seasoned rice. And it is very simple to do. Here is a recipe for something that goes well with any enchilada or burrito, or taco for that matter. And it takes only about half an hour to make.

Raw Materials

2 Tablespoons olive or corn oil

1 large white onion (peeled and chopped)

1 medium red pepper (diced)

2 cloves garlic (peeled and chopped very fine)

1 medium Jalapeno pepper (de-seeded and chopped)

or 2 small Chipotle peppers (dried or canned; if dried, reconstitute first)

1 teaspoon cumin

1 teaspoon coriander

1 teaspoon sea salt

1 12-ounce bottle of good Mexican lager

1 cup of long-grain white rice

1 15-ounce can of diced red tomatoes (don't drain)

Tools

large nonstick pot

knife

cutting board

1. Select a nonstick pot suitable for holding the expanded rice and assorted flavorings.

2. Heat the oil til it moves easily around the pot when the pot is slightly shaken.

3. Add the onion, garlic, and red peppers.

4. Sautee until the onions are translucent.

5. Add the spices, stir.

6. Add the beer, stir. Take a moment to savor the aroma!

7. Add the rice, stir.

8. Add the tomatoes and juice, stir again several times until the mixture delights the eye.

9. Reduce the heat to a low simmer and cook for 15-20 minutes, depending on your stove and how much juice was in the tomatoes, or how large of a sip you took of the beer before throwing it in.

Spicy Talk

From a woman's vantage, there is a major difference between spicy talk and vulgar talk. Guys really need to understand this difference. Particularly at the dinner table.

The analogy here is that adding spicy talk to your dinner conversation is like adding seasonings to a dish. Too much and you overwhelm or possibly offend; too little and it just seems out of place and awkward. The key to using seasonings and spicy talk is that both should embellish the overall theme, not become it.

Women often say that men walk with an attitude. Truth is, we talk with one too. For too many of us, our images of how we should talk to a woman are drawn from Hollywood scriptwriters who control the outcomes of their scenes, or from—as Zelda Fitzgerald once put it—"the philosophies of popular songs." Either way, our culture doesn't leave us much room for individuality. That, my friends, is one of the challenges of effective intimate communication. We have to learn how to be ourselves, against all the mediated odds.

One of the by-products of our mediated reliance on images is an over-reliance on bad language to assert our masculinity. For example, too many men rely on one word to express entirely too wide a range of feelings that should require other linguistic choices. The word, in case you haven't figured it out, begins with an "F" and rhymes with "luck." They use the word to express a desired sexual event (albeit one that, with that kind of attitude, is more about the assertion of dominance and power than love) as well as to cover a full range of despondencies, angers, fears, hatreds, and minor annoyances. The word, once uttered, is often addictive. We initially feel good saying it, so we say it again. We end up saying it too often, and too much. Sometimes we say it just to say it. Sometimes we repeat the word several times just to get into the phat rhythm of it, and sometimes we repeat it to emphasize something we've probably already forgotten. The word, like a virus, is also contagious. One guy says it to another guy, chances are good the other guy will fire it back. Then we both have it, and in too many cases, we've both lost it. Overall, the word is like swallowing a handful of cayenne pepper. It instantly burns the hell out of whatever, or whomever, it touches.

By contrast, there are many ways to be playful and creative with spices and with language. The more creative and playful you are with language, the more likely it is that you will become comfortable with yourself. You will be at home with your own enchilada.

The philosopher Martin Heidegger explains that men dwell within houses made out of words; Max Weber, another very bright guy, says that when we use language we a create "webs of significance that we ourselves have spun." Any way you look at it, we are *what*, and *how*, we speak. Our words are the spices that add—or detract—from the individual and collective themes of our lives.

Women know this to be true. That is part of the reason they listen to us. It is not so much they want to know what we are saying; they realize that what they are really listening to is *who we are*. This is called "listening between the lines" and intelligent women are very, very good at it.

If you want to be taken seriously as an individual, you need to learn how to speak as one. If you want your lady to see you as a creative person, you need to learn to use language to build that image. And if you want her to think of you as the most interesting, most special, and most intriguing man she has ever met, then, well, you probably have some serious work to do.

Spicy talk, properly used, can help you.

Like the appropriate use of seasonings, adding spice to your talk means developing the ways and means of embellishing and enlivening who are you. Spices and seasonings are like metaphors. Some are subtle, some nuanced, some overt, some bold, some pro-nounced. Some work well with others; others really need to be used alone. All of them require being carefully measured and well-adapted to the dishes being served.

Spicing Things Up

The entirely ordinary man uses salt and pepper, and little else. His language limits his vision just as his choice of spices limit his culinary horizon. His salt is a common curse; his pepper comes across as an unwanted leer. The extraordinary man, by comparison, has a wide variety of possibilities always available. His metaphors, as a result, are inspired.

Now how does this relate to conversation between women and men? What women want is a man who balances the ability to speak plainly and honestly with the ability to have fun with words and the dualities of their meanings. In other words, what women want is a man with a full array of spices and seasonings on hand, who knows how to use them, sparingly, to create new and imaginative possibilities for the relationship as well as for dinner.

I would like you reflect on that for awhile. While you are cooking. And perhaps, because of it.

THE RED MEAT AFFAIR

"I washed the potatoes, slit the tops, and wrapped
them in foil. I put them in the oven at five hundred
degrees... I took the steak out of its package,
stabbed it with a fork a zillion times on each side,
then sprinkled it with pepper and garlic powder and
soy sauce ...

(Later,) I took the steak off the grill. I put it on a plate
and stood in the night, looking at her. . . . We went
inside with the steak. I guess Cabo San Lucas and
the billfish would have to wait. The human heart
bears a greater urgency."

—Robert Crais, <u>Voodoo River</u>

Crimes Against the Heart

Fat, cholesterol, and cheap jokes aside, what do most men and women *really* want? Red meat. Period. A good grilled steak. Or a fork-tender, succulent pot roast.

But these days, men know just enough about the dangers of eating a steady diet of red meat not to. Many of us, therefore, have limited our intake of red meat so as to make its rare evening appearance on our dinner plate into a kind of culinary equivalent of a brief affair. A love affair. An affair of, and against, the heart.

Unless you are an avowed vegetarian—not that there is *anything wrong* with that—chances are pretty good that the occasional casual dalliance with a good steak, or a tender pot roast, or a tenderloin soup won't seriously deter your quest for health and longevity.

Women, unless they are also avowed vegetarians, also enjoy brief flings with red meat. Probably this is because a long, long time ago, a man who could provide meat for a romantic cave dweller's dinner was a man who could take care of his woman. And probably we are still left with genetic traces of this imprint.

Or maybe women just crave red meat because it tastes so damned good. I know that is my excuse.

The point of this chapter is admit, openly, publicly, that affairs with red meat are common in our culture. Rather than take the higher moral ground on this issue, I prefer to provide some cooking lessons designed to improve your skill in preparing and serving this seemingly deep-rooted food need. I figure if you are going to have an affair with red meat, you might as well do it right. And if you can't do it right, you shouldn't do it at all.

A Good Steak

There is nothing quite like a good steak, is there? I mean a *really* good steak. Say genuine Angus quality, about 1 ½" thick, cut from the tenderloin, grilled to perfection. Served after a salad, with a side of garlic or buttermilk mashed potatoes, sautéed mushrooms and/or grilled Vidalia onions . . . ah, now we are talking *real* food. Here is an affair to remember!

If this sounds like a meal you'd like to learn to cook, as well as one that might keep you from ever entering one of those chain steakhouses again, then my friend, read on. Learning to cook a good steak with all the trimmings is what this chapter is dedicated to.

On Angus Beef

When you go to the store to purchase your steak, buy only Angus certified beef. Why? Because Angus certification means that the highest industry and government standards for raising, processing, curing, and packaging the meat have been thoroughly met.

You're thinking: So what? Well, in layman's terms, this means simply that you can grill, sauté, broil, or roast any cut of Angus certified beef safely *below* temperatures reserved for lesser quality cuts. Even more simply: you can cook your steak medium, medium rare, or even rare, without fear of dying from some gawd-awful bacterial infection.

That's what.

I still wouldn't eat it raw, and neither should you. The days of steak tartar are *over*, pal.

Green Peppercorn-Encrusted Ribeye or Tenderloin Steak with Garlic Mashed Potatoes, Grilled Vidalia Onions, and Sautéed Tarragon (or not) Mushrooms

The art of grilling or sautéing (e.g., pan-frying) a good steak is a relatively simple one. Any fool can toss a piece of meat on a hot fire, watch it sizzle, and when it appears sufficiently black, fling it onto a plate. This is not, however, artful. Nor is it wise. Wise men know that the Tao of a Good Steak means knowing how to prepare it prior to grilling, knowing what approximate temperature to use, knowing how long it should take, and, finally, knowing how to finish the steak prior to serving it to a special red-meat loving guest.

Raw Materials

Two 1 ½"–thick Angus steaks (Tenderloin; Ribeye; Porterhouse)

½ .50-ounce jar of freeze-dried green peppercorns (coarsely ground)

1/8 of a 16-ounce bottle of Dale's sauce

5 good-sized Russet potatoes (washed, skinned, and chopped)

Water for boiling

5 cloves garlic (peeled and chopped)

¼ lb. White Vermont Cheddar Cheese (grated)

Sea salt and black Java pepper to taste

½ lb white or Crimini mushrooms (wiped clean and quartered)

1 Tablespoon extra virgin olive oil

Dash tarragon (optional)

2 Vidalia onions (skinned, but otherwise intact)

Dash dried basil

Dash dried oregano

Dash of black Java pepper

Couple of drops of olive oil

Tools

good heavy frying pan or grill

large pot

skillet

grinder

knife

cutting board

colander

large mixing bowl

The Blueprint

1. Allow your beef to reach room temperature (assuming your room is normally air-conditioned) for about 30-minutes prior to cooking.

2. Meanwhile, select five good-sized Russet potatoes, skin them, and slice them into 2" chunks suitable for boiling.

3. Cover with water, add a handful of ice cubes (to keep them white), and cover the pot.

4. Clean your electric coffee mill by unplugging it, wiping a damp cloth around both the blade area and the plastic top, and then wiping again with a dry paper towel. You don't want old coffee grounds to mix in with your peppercorns. Empty half of the jar of peppercorns into a coffee-grinder and hit the pulse button three times or until a coarse cut has been achieved.

5. About fifteen minutes prior to cooking the steaks, press the pepper-corns into each side of the meat and enjoy the wild aromatics of this mix.

6. Turn on the stove and bring the potato water to boil. When it achieves that state, cut the heat back to low simmer and set the timer for 10 minutes.

7. Go outside and light your gas grill or other, lesser fire. Set the dials to "High" to establish your manly authority over the elements that are still under our control. Shout something unintelligible at the local trees while you are at it. This is meat eating, and deserves to bring out all those male hormones. Look down. If your grill is smoking, you need to lower the fire and use one of those commercially available wire brushes to clean it. Do this *before* you cook the steak, fool. You don't want last week's plum-marinade from the chicken wings to interfere with the Total Steak Presence we are achieving here.

8. Go back inside and quarter the mushrooms.

9. Place a sauté skillet on the stove and add a little olive oil to it. Let it sit there. Don't add the mushrooms to the skillet until you are ready to cook them, which will be after the steaks are done.

10. Place the two onions on two squares of tin foil. Drop some olive oil on the tops of each onion, and then toss on a dash of the spices. Get your hands into it, massaging the oil and spices into the skins of these sweet beasts. Pull the tin foil from the bottom-up and turn the tops clockwise to lock in the flavors.

11. Wash your hands. Place the onions on the grill. If you didn't wash you hands, chances are good that your hands are on fire now, too. Make sure the heat is now set at medium or medium-low, depend-ing on how hot your grill normally is.

12. Grill the onions from now until whenever the steaks are done. This could range from 15-45 minutes, depending on a wide variety of things that I don't want to go into here. In general, 30 minutes is about right for grilled onions.

13. Ask her how she likes her steak cooked. *Don't guess.* If you like your steak medium to medium rare, then allow about 8-10 minutes per side over a low flame (the only temperature to cook a steak). Turn twice during the cooking process at these intervals: 4-5 minutes on the top side, another 4-5 minutes on the bottom side; a second 4 minutes during which time you baste the top side with Dale's sauce; a second 4 minutes during which time you baste the bottom side with Dale's sauce. You can use a knife to cut into the thickest part of each steak to test its doneness, or you can rely on your experience, or you can guess. Notice how I arranged the last sentence in descending order of certitude? Just how certain do you need to be, tonight? Go with it, pal.

14. Remove the steaks from the grill and turn the grill off. Leave the onions on there, cooking in the leftover heat. Make sure the cover is closed.

15. Place the steaks in the microwave or oven; really, any small enclosed space will do. This will keep them warm while you prepare the mashed potatoes and mushrooms.

16. Drain the cooked potatoes in a colander. *Thoroughly* drain them, unless you favor watery mashed potatoes.

17. Transfer the *thoroughly* drained potatoes to a large mixing bowl, add the garlic and cheese, a palmful of sea salt, whatever amount of pepper you need to fulfill your dreams, and mix on medium for 30-60 seconds. You want them to be slightly stiff and maybe even a little lumpy. These are Manly Mashed Potatoes, and it should show. In my opinion, they also taste better this way. If you want the creamier, unlumped kind, just add about ½ cup of milk or butter-milk and mix for another minute or so. Transfer to your serving bowl. Make sure there is a serving spoon in it.

18. Heat the awaiting oil in the skillet on high. Add the 'shrooms and maybe a dash of tarragon and black pepper. Cook just long enough to see the white turn to light brown, or about 1 ½ - 2 minutes. If you cook any longer the mushrooms will give up their natural juices and taste like it, too. Transfer the 'shrooms immediately to the steak plate, on top of, and surrounding, the perfectly made steaks. Place on the table.

19. Go outside and retrieve the onions—use an insulated glove—serving them on the individual plates in their burnt tin foil wrappers or naked. You choose, it's your date or friend or wife, and you should at least know how she likes her grilled onions served. You don't? Well, then, just ask her. This isn't rocket science.

I serve this steak with a hearty red wine, preferably a Cabernet Sauvignon, California Red Zinfadel, or Merlot. Other men I know wouldn't serve a steak with anything other than beer. But they always are the guys who are unlucky in love, as they say. So it goes.

On the Barry Bell Method

Barry Bell is an actor friend of mine, a guy you've seen a million times playing hard guys, cops, and desperadoes on TV movies and regularly scheduled programs. He is also an expert chef and damn fine blues guitarist.

The Barry Bell Method of doing a steak begins by grinding your green peppercorns by hand, using only a mortar and pestle, which will probably be much the amazement of your guest.

Only a mortar and pestle will do. Probably he is right. But this is the same guy who will only make this steak in the time-honored pan-fried tradition ("grilling is for the meek"), and who believes it is perfectly acceptable to top the cooked meat with a thin layer of Boursin cheese.

And that's the secret of the Barry Bell Method. Hand-grinding, pan-frying, and melted Boursin on top. Anyone who has dined at his table on this feast can, and no doubt will, say that his method is delicious beyond words. If you care about fat, it's also a little over-the-top.

But I say if you are going to have a dangerous red meat affair, you might as well be willing to go all the way, right?

On *Dale's Sauce*

My old pal and guitar-playing buddy, Drew Thompson, introduced me to Dale's sauce via the original Dale's restaurant in Florence, Alabama. Drew and I were the lead and rhythm aces back in those days for the legendary Whitedog band (you can read all about it in my 1991 book, *Living in the Rock n Roll Mystery,* published by Southern Illinois University Press). We used to hang out a lot in the Muscle Shoals area, specifically at Muscle Shoals Sound. This is the place, by the way, where Percy Sledge recorded his classic, "When a Man Loves a Woman," which I've always found to be a very fine tune to fire up while grilling.

Dale's was the best restaurant in town, and Abernathy was by far its best waiter. We'd go there before playing at one of the local bars or hanging out and talking music at the studio, and Abernathy would instruct us in the fine art of cooking and serving tenderloins. The trick, as I've noted here, is to baste the steaks with Dale's immediately before (if you aren't using peppercorns) or during the last stage of their cooking.

Why Dale's? Try it, you'll see. The proof is in the flavor. It doesn't cover up the natural goodness of the beef, merely "brings it to a full musical presence," as Abernathy used to say.

An Honorable Pot Roast

It is surprising to me to find men who love a good pot roast, but have no idea how to prepare one. I wonder what other parts of their lives suffer from the same lack of initiative, or even basic skill. In truth, there is no good reason *not* to learn how to put together a roast beef dinner. It is easy to prepare (only one large pot is used), requires no attention whatsoever while cooking, and delights anyone who enters the house while it is being made. Unless you are a total pig, a good-sized roast and the attendant veggies will make enough leftovers to carry you through an otherwise tight budgetary week.

Pot roast is, however, much more than just an easy meal to make. It is symbolic of a well-ordered life. To serve pot roast is an honorable thing, a way of turning lusty red meat into a well-made, properly turned-out roast. It is an affair, to be sure, but an affair largely consummated with our mythic past. It reminds us of Sunday dinners Mom used to make. It hints of a time when men were men and women were proud of it. It takes us back to a time that was simpler, to a world that was simpler, to a life that had time enough in it for the simple pleasures to be enough.

The Red Meat Affair

Learn to make this dish. It will improve your memory of things past. And it will enhance your chances of demonstrating your honor.

Raw Materials

2-3 lb sirloin tip roast

2 Tablespoons good quality olive oil

1 large onion (peeled)

3-4 carrots (peeled)

6-8 small red potatoes (scrubbed)

1 15-ounce can beef broth

1 28-ounce can diced tomatoes

1 cup Burgundy or Beaujolais red wine

6 whole cloves

1 bay leaf

2 cloves garlic (peeled and diced)

2 Tablespoons dried parsley (or 1/2 cup of fresh parsley)

Sea salt and black Java pepper to taste

Tools

large roaster

knife

cutting board

The Blueprint

1. Preheat oven to 350 degrees.

2. Run the roast under cold water for 10-15 seconds to remove any blood. Pat dry with a clean towel. Rub sea salt and black pepper into the meat with your hands.

3. Select a large, oven-proof casserole or large pot with a tight-fitting lid.

4. Heat the oil in the casserole unit until hot over medium-high heat.

5. Add the sirloin roast. It will sizzle; be careful. Brown the meat on all sides.

6. Add the beef broth, wine, and diced tomatoes. Stir.

7. Add the bay leaf, garlic, and parsley. Stir again. Cover.

8. Bring to simmer over medium-high heat.

9. While you are waiting for the liquids to boil, push the cloves into the onion.

10. Place the onion on top of the roast and spoon the now simmering liquids over the onion.

11. Cover and remove from heat.

12. Put the casserole unit, with the tight-fitting lid firmly in place, into the oven.

13. Bake for 2 1/2 hours.

14. Remove the casserole unit and stir the veggies and the liquids. Put the unit back into the oven, this time *uncovered*. Bake for 1 hour. Most of the liquids will have evaporated or been absorbed by the veggies and meat.

Serve on a large platter. Place the roast (it will be fork-tender) in the center of the platter and surround with the veggies. Quarter the clove-spiced onion. Accompany with the same kind of red wine you cooked the meat in, and large quantities of thick-sliced sourdough bread.

Steak and Spinach Soup

Soup, like a good home-spun story, is a comfort food. It is the kind of meal that suggests a kind of wholesome at-home narrative, a staple story from the family kitchen. Yet, at the same time, with the right ingredients, soup can transcend its homey genre. It can tease and induce the palate to new ways of responding to its substance, to its sense of style.

Steak soup is just such a dish. Our friends Anne and Lacy Flora taught us to prepare this new version of a classic wholesome soup. Lacy is the man of the house, and the chief cook. On a crisp autumn evening it is *just* the thing!

Raw Materials

1 lb of beef tenderloin (thinly sliced and then cut into bite-sized pieces)

1 Tablespoon Extra Virgin Olive Oil

3 carrots (peeled and thinly sliced)

2 lbs of fresh spinach (thoroughly washed, de-stemmed, and hand shredded)

2 15-ounce cans beef broth

dry sherry

Tools

large soup pot

knife

cutting board

The Blueprint

1. Sauté the tenderloin in the oil in a large pot over medium heat.

2. Add the carrots and continue sautéing for one minute.

3. Add the beef broth. Stir. Cover the pot.

4. Reduce heat to low. Allow to cook for 20-30 minutes, or until you are ready to serve.

5. Add the spinach, stir twice, and cover the pot.

6. Cook for one additional minute, or until the spinach has shriveled sufficiently to look like it belongs in a soup.

Pour 1 ounce of dry sherry into the bottom of each soup bowl. Add some broth and a generous helping of steak, spinach, and carrot. Serve with warm dinner rolls.

The Stakes in Relational Talk

Many men I know say that there is no such thing as an innocent date. And no, they are not talking badly about their choice of women. What they mean is that these days the stakes are higher than they used to be. And "used to be" wasn't that long ago.

What they mean is that most women are interested in only one thing: developing a long-term relationship. Anything less is unacceptable. Frankly, that is a lot less scary to me that what my dear old dad told me women wanted, which was, and I quote, "your money and your balls." So from my vantage, the stakes have always been high. Ironically, when I ask women if this is true—that what they really want is a long-term relationship—the answer is usually "no." Women want all kinds of things—someone who is fun to be with, someone who makes them laugh, someone they can trust, someone to be their lover, someone to be a friend, etc. Rarely do they meet someone who fulfills all of their needs. So no, guys, hooking you ain't necessarily what they want.

Similarly, when women ask: what do men want? The answer is equally bizarre. Well, we are dogs after all, right? After only one thing? Here again, when I ask men what they want from a relationship, sex isn't that high on their collective list. Men, like women, want all kinds of things, and even many of the same things. But they do not always want sex. And if that is all they want, chances are pretty good they aren't getting any.

Ladies and gentlemen, we have a common problem. And that problem has to do with how we talk *to* each other *about* each other. And what we think about, but don't say, or what assumptions about the opposite sex we bring to the table. And while we are on the subject, let's not forget how we have learned to perceive—or should I say, *mis*perceive—each other and our motives. Research studies now demonstrate that *mis*communication—not communication—is the basis of most of our relationships. Put simply, we don't understand each other most of the time.

The fact is women and men don't know how to talk honestly with each other about what we want. The reason for this sad state of affairs is that nobody ever taught us how to. We spent years sitting in straight rows learning advanced math, algebra, trigonometry, and physics, but precious little time developing our *relational communication* understandings and skills. No wonder we miscommunicate!

Some time ago a research partner of mine and I conducted a study to explore how women and men develop these patterns of miscommunication. What we found out, and published, was striking. In early adolescence, during the time when men and women begin dating and exploring the intimate relational dance, two things happen. Women are led to believe that their purpose is to be desirable to men, and men are led to believe that our purpose is to thrive on undifferentiated lust. Nowhere during this period are we encouraged to talk to each other openly and honestly about these feelings, these cultural learnings, these destructive fictions of our collective imagination.

We also learn to be self-centered in relationships. If we form a close relationship with an intimate other, our well-intentioned parents try to break it up. We are told there are "too many fish in the sea," and other largely inappropriate and offensive metaphors that reduce the complexity of our feelings to mere carnal desire. If we resist that logic, we are ridiculed as being "immature," or "foolish." Our love is at best "puppy love."

No wonder we learn to enter relationships warily and exit them when our needs are not being met. No wonder our culture is one in which the "serial relationship phenomenon" is truly the relational law of the land. And no wonder that we grow up, or just get older, still clinging to misperceptions, misunderstandings, and miscommunication about and with each other.

This has to change.

Look, I *know*. I know personal relationships are difficult. I know that beyond the playfulness is the inevitable sex question, and that beyond that is the relational issue. Beyond that may be heaven on earth, or hell; chances are it will be a bit of both.

I know, as you probably do, that if you are murdered, it will more than likely be by someone very close to you, and more often than not, your relational partner. I know that people say things to each other that not even a lifetime of apologies and gifts can overcome, things that murder wouldn't even resolve. And I know that sometimes the best parts of being in love have some relationship to pain. How else would you recognize it?

But we do *need* satisfying relationships. We cannot live fully without them.

We are talking stakes and steaks here. What began as a possible affair has become something else entirely.

So what should you do?

I suggest that you talk regularly and honestly about your feelings with each other. Do this, however, knowing that it won't be easy. Digesting a big steak dinner isn't easy on your system, either. Maintain your sense of humor. Treat each other with profound respect. Really listen to what is being said, and to what can't quite be. Don't always go for closure; this isn't a sales call. Intimate relationships are intricate processes, they evolve and change over time.

Realize that women and men *are* eternally different. This doesn't mean you can't ever understand each other, only that you will understand some of the same things *differently*. For example, it is important to begin that conversation with the knowledge that women prefer to define the status of a relationship while men prefer not to. As I have said before, women always take the longer view. We typically have trouble thinking beyond the weekend. This gender difference will rear its head during this particular conversation, perhaps in surprising ways.

You don't have to fear it, or be annoyed by it. Certainly you shouldn't treat the whole issue as if it shouldn't be one. It *is* one. Deal with it. Deal with it as a difference that matters. This isn't about power, about one of you being "right" and the other one being "wrong"; it certainly isn't just about *you*, either. You are probably selfish enough in every other aspect of your life, so you don't have to be that way in this one.

Nobody can tell you what to say except that little man that lives inside of you, the one who tells you how you really feel. The one you too often ignore. And the one you wish you didn't ignore, after the fact. Listen to your little man. He knows you better than the rest of you put together.

He's the guy who ordered the steak, remember? The stakes in any intimate relationship *are* high. I don't need to go into the more frightening viral details. Although our sex is famous for living in denial, we simply don't have time or the luxury for that anymore.

I know what you are thinking. You are thinking that I've suddenly become very serious in what had been a rather irreverent cookbook. Is this any place for *that*? Hey, isn't the reason you bought this book (or someone close to you bought it for you) is to teach you a thing or two about cooking?

That is precisely what I am doing. If you like red meat, you need to be aware of the costs. Of what's really at stake with a steak. Or an honorable roast. Even a steak and spinach soup. If you choose to go ahead with it, with this little culinary affair, then by all means, do it right!

And don't say you didn't know what you were getting into. You do, and you did. The one thing you never want to say is that it wasn't worth it. Make it worth it. Learn how to cook the red meat right. Learn how to talk honestly, and openly, about what you really want.

DIALOGIC CHICKEN

"After they made love, Bosch went into the kitchen to open a bottle of beer and make dinner. He peeled an onion and chopped it up along with a green pepper. He then cleared the cutting board into a frying pan and sauteed the mixture with butter, powdered garlic and other seasonings. He added two chicken breasts and cooked them until the meat was easy to shred and pull away from the bone with a fork. He added a can of Italian tomato sauce, a can of crushed tomatoes and more seasonings. He finished by pouring a shot of red wine from Eleanor's bottle in. While it all simmered, he put a pot of water on to boil the rice... It was the best dinner he knew how to cook in a kitchen."

—Michael Connelly, Trunk Music

Coming Back to Chicken

Here's an astounding Dr. Bud fact that may surprise you: Men discovered the joys of cooking chicken long before the contemporary horde of white lab-coated nutritionists announced that it was good for us. In those good ol' days, men prepared a wide variety of chicken dishes—some done in marinates, some with sauces—and we called those manly feasts "Barbecue."

True, many of our homemade marinades were long on oils and sugars and short on creative flavors, but we liked them anyway. To fully breathe in the aroma of a well-prepared and slathered chicken breast, leg, or thigh roasting on an open fire was a manly rite of passage. It was something fathers taught sons how to do. It was something good that women would grudgingly admit about us: "Well, Henry isn't much in the kitchen, but he sure can make a *fine* barbecued chicken."

> Women often speak indirectly. They say one thing, but really mean another. As confounding as this practice can be, it is also part of their charm, part of their mystery. It is my personal belief that this female statement about what Henry can "do," as well as how well he "does it" (e.g., note the adjective, *fine*), should be understood as an intimate metaphor.

Over the years I have witnessed many such *in vivo* performances of this line by women. When combined with a true understanding of their nonverbal actions while uttering it—the slow bodily sway back and forth, the arms crossed softly just beneath their breasts, the wicked little smile that bespeaks some kind of earlier surrender, the afterglow unmistakably centered in their eyes—I have more or less satisfied my initial hypothesis.

Dialogic Chicken

With these suggestive words and their accompanying bodily movement and gesture, they are, and are not, speaking about chicken. And it's the "not" part that is the key to understanding the "are" part. What I am saying here, in layman's terms, is that Henry is giving her what she really wants: a good meal that leads to a deeper, more intimate ... well, shall we say, *dialogue*?

Chicken is *dialogic*. Unlike other prepared meats that inspire different associations (e.g., a steak's hot, naked, aggressiveness or marinated pork's deep-down and dirty hoggliness), when women and men enjoy chicken together, they tend to talk themselves into a higher and more mutual state of Being. They become closely connected; they begin to understand that feelings of mutual intimate connectedness are part of the more general poetry and mystery of the stars. Listen closely to what "gets said" the next time you "do" chicken together. Now listen to what is *not* being said. What goes on in-between the lines is what makes all the difference.

This word magic only works, of course, if you want it to. Otherwise, you are just eating chicken. Is this what you want? I don't think so. My friends, you have to be able to *imagine* a better world before you can enter it. What I am passing along to you in this book is more valuable than just recipes: it is a way to think differently about food. It is a way to imagine it in connection to your most intimate relationships and to your communication in those relationships. It is designed to help you act, creatively, on that which you imagine.

The good news is that chicken preparation accomplished by men isn't limited to barbecue anymore. In the last two decades, chicken has come into its own. For many Americans, chicken comprises more than half of our weekly meat consumption and for some it is the only meat we *ever* eat. Non-vegan vegetarians have even been known to backslide from their sacred roots-and-berries routines when a savory chicken dish is offered to them.

Why is this? Why is chicken so universally appealing? Is it just because of its relative healthiness? I don't think so.

It is because the chicken—which, in its natural state, is little more than a rather ridiculous-looking and ridiculous-acting barnyard fowl capable of little more than laying eggs—is, in truth, the veritable embodiment of the basic love humans have for dramatic *transformation*. Properly plucked and minimally processed, the chicken moves initially from mindless and chaotic clucking to a liminal stage of quietude and readiness; from there, what the chicken becomes depends on how well the cook's creative imagination and skill merges with the raw materials of this made-to-cook bird.

One kind of transformation tends to lead to, or inspire, others. A simple chicken dinner can often become the basis for talk between possibly consenting adults about the very possibilities of said consent. The low groans of delight offered by a tasty chicken dish can be read as a sign of a deeper, as yet unfulfilled, need. As Dr. Bud often sez, "one thing always leads to another."

For this reason, chicken should be approached as a vessel for communicating the creative richness in the mysterious, often ineffable, dialogue that is the heart of love between humans. Men who learn to master the art of unlocking the flavors of a finely cooked chicken may find that they have also stumbled onto a metaphor for unlocking the hearts of their dearly intended. Such is often the case. For this reason, the recipes I offer here are admittedly a little dangerous . . . this isn't just a chicken we are preparing anymore, is it?

**Perfectly Fine Honey-Mustard Chicken for New Cooks, or
Baked Chicken in a Bag**

I begin this section with a recipe that could be subtitled "Chicken for Dummies." All it requires of any guy is the ability to place an unwrapped chicken into a plastic baking bag, add 1 tablespoon of flour (to prevent the bag from exploding during the cooking process), add virtually any assortment of raw vegetables, close the bag, and pop it into the oven for the prescribed time on the baking bag box.

I've livened up this basic approach in order to improve the relative intelligence of the overall operation. It makes a wonderful first bird for the man new to the kitchen, and a lovely dinner for two. Try it, you'll be amazed at how easy it is to make a perfectly fine meal.

 Raw Materials

1 3-5 lb whole chicken (unwrapped and washed off under cold water; or you can use already cut-up pieces, if you prefer)

½ cup of honey

¼ cup Dijon-style mustard

1 baking bag (medium is for chickens of this size) and baking bag tie

1 Tablespoon flour (any white, all-purpose or unbleached kind)

3-4 stalks of celery (cut into quarters)

5-6 whole carrots, sliced into large pieces (or 10 baby carrots left whole)

1 medium onion, chopped into quarters

Sea salt and black Java pepper to taste

Tools

baking bag (available on the paper aisle of the grocery store)

roasting pan, cookie sheet, or large baking dish

The Blueprint

1. Preheat oven to 325 degrees.

2. Unwrap the bird and hold under cold running water for 15-30 seconds. Pat dry with paper towels. Lay on paper towels.

3. Wash your hands thoroughly.

4. Blend the mustard into the honey with a large spoon. Taste it. If you want to add more mustard, go ahead.

5. Pour the mixture over the chicken and rub into the skin with your bare hands.

6. Put the chicken into the baking bag. Do NOT lick your fingers!! Uncooked chicken is loaded with potentially deadly bacteria. If you lick your fingers after you've rubbed the honey mustard into the skin, you will certainly become very sick and may actually die. No kidding. Take this warning *very* seriously.

7. Now go wash your hands again. This time, *thoroughly.*

8. Add the remaining ingredients, and close with the baking bag tie.

9. Cut 4-5 slits into the top of the baking bag.

10. Place on a cookie sheet or baking dish, and put into the oven.

11. Set the timer for the length of time specified on the baking bag box. Go relax. Take a shower. Listen to some good music. Muse on the Ultimate Nature of Persons and Things. Read Giovanni Baccaccio's classic tale "How to Put the Devil into Hell." Or a Barry Hannah short story.

12. When the timer sounds, remove the bird from the oven, and then from the bag. The bag will have contained most of the heat, so be careful.

13. Slice the bag down the middle with a sharp knife or pair of kitchen sissors, allow the steam to escape. To test for doneness, cut into the thick end of the breast; if the juices run clear, your bird is cooked. If it isn't, remove from the bag, place back on the baking dish (without the veggies; they will be done), and place back into the oven for another 10 minutes or so. In most cases, 10 minutes will be enough. If it takes longer than this, chances are good you made a mistake reading the poundage label on the chicken (and therefore miscalculated the time needed), or your oven is turned off. If neither of these explanations applies, then purchase one of those little oven thermometers and place it into your oven to test the temperature. To do this, turn the oven to 350 and, after five minutes, see what the gauge says. Trust the gauge. Adjust your cooking times accordingly.

Two Ways to Cook Chicken in a Crock Pot

A crock pot is a large porcelain container that provides slow, even heating to anything put inside of it. It requires a minimum of moisture, since slow-cooking produces liquids from the ingredients that are constantly recirculated within the pot. It requires a minimum of effort, because all you need to do is fill the pot with whatever you are cooking in the morning, turn the heat on low, and it will cook all day without any assistance from you. And it is virtually fool-proof, which means any guy can use it successfully.

I think you should own a crock pot. Here are two very good reasons why.

Crock Pot Chicken I: Chicken and Veggies

This is an excellent first-time crock pot user recipe. My guess is you will like the result so much that it will become a staple in your home.

 Raw Material

1 package of chicken (whole or cut-up chicken, boneless breasts, thighs, whatever)

1 large onion (peeled and sliced or chopped)

2-3 stalks of celery (washed and chopped)

3-4 carrots (peeled and sliced) or 10-12 baby carrots (washed)

1 15-ounce can 99% fat-free chicken broth

1 teaspoon dried basil or 1 whole basil leaf

1 teaspoon green capers (optional, but worth it)

Sea salt and black Java pepper to taste

Optional: 3-4 Russet potatoes (peeled and chopped)

Dialogic Chicken

crock pot

knife

cutting board

The Blueprint

1. Line the bottom of the crock pot with the onions and celery.

2. Place the chicken on top of the vegetables.

3. Sprinkle the chicken with the basil or lay the whole leaf over the center of the bird.

4. Add the capers.

5. Salt and pepper to taste.

6. Toss in the carrots.

7. Pour the chicken broth over the meat and vegetables. If you are adding the potatoes, do it now.

8. Sprinkle a little more pepper on top. Cover.

9. Turn the heat on low.

10. Return in 7-9 hours, open the cover. Serve.

If you are not cooking the potatoes with the chicken, serve this dish with some steamed white or brown rice. Any decent mild white wine (such as Chenin Blanc) will make a fine accompaniment.

Crock Pot Chicken II: Chicken and Black Olive Tangine

Here is an exotic dish whose roots may be found in North Africa. It is easy to make in a crock pot because "tangine" or "tangia" is a round dish with a conical lid fashioned out of earthenware, which is very similar to today's porcelain crock pot knock-off. The aroma of slow-baked chicken, cilantro, black olives, and lemon alone will impress your guest, but the flavor is—as they say in L.A.—to *die* for.

Raw Materials

1 package of chicken (I use breasts, but you can select any whole, cut-up, or selection of pieces you like)

2 Tablespoons fresh garlic (peeled and chopped)

½ cup fresh parsley (de-stemmed and chopped)

½ cup fresh cilantro (de-stemmed and chopped)

1 teaspoon ground cumin

I teaspoon good quality olive oil

2-4 Tablespoons lemon juice (quantity depends on how much chicken you are using)

1 Tablespoon black Java pepper

1 large onion (peeled and finely sliced, then diced)

1 15-ounce can 99% fat-free chicken broth

1 lemon (washed and thinly sliced)

1 jar of Kalamata black olives

Sea salt and pepper to taste

Dialogic Chicken

Tools

crock pot

food processor

knife

cutting board

The Blueprint

1. Combine the garlic, parsley, cilantro, cumin, olive oil, 1 tablespoon of the lemon juice, and pepper in the bowl of a food processor. Turn on the food processor for 15 seconds.

2. Turn off the food processor, scrape the sides, and turn on again for 5 seconds, or until the mixture forms a kind of slimy paste.

3. Rub the chicken pieces thoroughly with this paste.

4. Place the onion slices and chicken broth in the bottom of the crock pot.

5. Layer the chicken pieces on top. Cover with the olives, lemon juice, and lemon slices. Don't worry about what it looks like. Trust me.

6. Cover and cook on low for 7-9 hours.

Avoid the temptation to lift the lid, even though the aroma will call to you, much like the Sirens did to Ulysses. Why not lift the lid? Because crock pots do not recover their heat very quickly, and this will interrupt the slow cooking, even-heating process. Serve with a side of saffron (see On Saffron Rice) rice and warm pita bread.

On Saffron Rice

You could buy some real saffron, but at $15 per ounce, it is very expensive. Or you could purchase a packet of commercially-available Yellow Rice, which is wonderful stuff and makes a sensible substitute. Follow the package directions. Garnish with a little fresh parsley when you serve.

A Warm, Tender, and Entirely Well-Roasted Sunday Bird

You probably recall Sunday dinners at home from your now-mythical childhood. You know, the one where you were always the perfectly well-behaved child? The one where you starred in all sports? Got all A's? Yeah, that one.

My guess is that in addition to making things up, you ate a lot of roasted chicken. My guess is also that you recall those dinners fondly now, not just because of the chicken, but because of the dialogue inspired by sharing chicken together. You needed the honest dialogue to balance the things you were making up about yourself. And you still do. You've just never conceived of it that way before. Do so now.

The basic idea behind roasting a bird is to let the natural flavor of the chicken emerge through the cooking process. Do not to try to mess with it too much. Avoid loading up the fowl with exotic spices and seasonings. For honest dialogue to emerge over roasted chicken, timeless spices that have been shared between women and men—I am speaking about salt and pepper here—are enough. A fresh basil leaf or two is welcome, but only if you and your dinner companion know each other pretty well already. Anything more is likely to lead to a long evening that ends with a monologue, not dialogue.

Dialogic Chicken

Raw Materials

3 – 4 ½ lb whole chicken (as fresh as possible or at least with skin that is not yellowed)

1 medium onion, preferably Vidalia, but *not* a red onion (peeled and left whole)

1 bunch of fresh parsley (washed)

Sea salt and black Java pepper

Tools

roasting pan

The Blueprint

1. Preheat your oven to 425 degrees and lower the shelf in your oven to accommodate the bird.

2. Unwrap the chicken and run under cold water. Fill the cavity with cold water to rinse out any leftover blood.

3. Pat dry with paper towels.

4. Cut off the extra fat at both ends of the bird.

5. Insert the peeled onion and parsley into the bird's cavity.

6. Rub a handful of salt and pepper all over the body of the bird.

7. Place the bird on a roasting pan in the middle of the oven.

8. Roast at 425 degrees until it is done (about 20 minutes per pound).

9. When the timer goes off, remove the cooked bird from the oven and allow it to stand for 10 minutes; carve and serve with your side dishes.

While the bird is roasting, prepare your side dishes. Keep them simple. You want the center of attention to be your dialogue, not your vegetables. I recommend parslied new potatoes and lightly steamed French-style green beans, but choose whatever you like. Buttered carrots are good. Steamed broccoli. Whatever. Round out the dinner with a loaf of warm bread. This meal can be accompanied by any good quality white wine; I like a California Chardonnay. But its essence is so pure that a good cold glass of milk will do.

During dinner, open the dialogue by speaking about the relationship of the day's activities to those eternal good questions about our purpose and meaning: What is our nature? What are we here for? If the chicken is right, this will lead to talk about deeper poetic and relational matters, which, in turn, can and very likely should lead elsewhere, to something more intimate than chocolate, more complex than cognac.

You can figure it out.

On Timers

Probably you should set the automatic timer for the desired length of time. You never want to scorch your bird. The skin will be blackened and the dark meat will still be almost raw. Do it my way. Do it the right way.

Basic technique: After the first 30 minutes, baste the bird with its own juices every 15 minutes.

Advanced technique: Melt a stick of unsalted butter in your micro-wave (30 seconds on High). Brush or spoon over the bird every 15 minutes. If you are feeling particularly adept, add some slivers of garlic to the butter.

Grilled (or Sautéed) Chicken

Dialogue is all about taking risks, being profoundly open to differences, and yet being able to maintain a preferred—but let us hope, an enlightened—point of view.

Taking risks with chicken means moving beyond simple oven roasting. Frying chicken is an option. So is sautéing. My favorite alternative method for attaining dialogue, however, is *grilling* chicken. Why? Because when it comes to chicken, I fundamentally believe in the transformative capacities of marinades coupled with an open fire. This is my unwavering and preferred point of view on chickens, and it has allowed me to grow considerably as a cook as well as a person. Marinades are all about being open to differences, and to taking risks. Yet, at the same time, they reveal a deeper pattern of purpose and method.

Allow me to demonstrate how you can apply this knowledge.

What I do below is to create a *basic pattern* for marinating chicken (see "The Basic Pattern" paragraph below); I then develop a table of *alternative marinades*, each one capable of appealing to an ever-broadening understanding of the possibilities of difference. Once you have mastered these marinades, try using your experience, the basic pattern, and your imagination to create your own!

All the recipes listed below work exceptionally well when you grill or sauté the chicken.

> To grill, simply place the boneless chicken pieces on the grill over a medium-to-low fire. Turn after 3-4 minutes. After another 3-4 minutes have passed, your chicken will be done. Remove from grill.

To sauté the chicken, heat your skillet on medium-high until a drop of water dances on the surface. Drop each boneless chicken piece onto the skillet and cook for 3-4 minutes per side. Remove from pan.

On Marinades

To marinade, simply combine the ingredients, pour over the chicken pieces, and allow to soak in the refrigerator for 2-3 hours, or even overnight. All marinates are combinations of three key elements: *penetrants* (e.g., vinegar, lemon juice, soy sauce, mustard, wine, etc.); *lubricants* (e.g., olive oil, vegetable oil, honey, yogurt, or molasses); *spices and seasonings* (e.g., garlic, peppers, etc.). To make any marinade, just combine the ingredients and stir thoroughly. To use any marinade, just pour what you've just stirred over the chicken, turn the chicken pieces to coat evenly, cover, and refrigerate. Pretty easy, huh?

I am assuming that you will be marinating 2 boneless chicken breasts or 12 chicken wings for each of the recipes below. If you are preparing more than that, adjust the ingredients accordingly. Remember, you need to have enough marinade to cover a *single layer* of chicken pieces in a glass baking dish. The recipes below show the marinade ingredients and suggested side dishes for the type of chicken you are creating.

Exotic Oriental Chicken with Mixed Oriental Veggies, Sesame Cucumbers, and White rice

½ cup of plum wine

1 Tablespoon red wine vinegar

1 Tablespoon soy sauce or tamari

¼ cup molasses

½ teaspoon onion powder

1 clove of garlic, minced

1 teaspoon ground or grated ginger

Dialogic Chicken

All-South Rebel Chicken with Green Onion Potato Salad, Cornbread, and Sandra's Signature Salad

> ½ cup balsamic vinegar
>
> 2 Tablespoons Dale's sauce
>
> 1 Tablespoon Dijon mustard
>
> ¼ cup peanut oil
>
> 2 cloves garlic, minced
>
> 1 teaspoon black Java pepper
>
> ¼ teaspoon cayenne

San Franciscan Harbor Chicken with Roasted Root Veggies, Succotash, or Fresh Ears of Corn

> 2 Tablespoons soy sauce or tamari
>
> ¼ cup coarse-ground Dijon-style mustard
>
> 1 Tablespoon extra-virgin olive oil
>
> 1 Tablespoon honey
>
> 2-3 cloves garlic, minced
>
> 1 Tablespoon ground or grated ginger

Connecticut Yankee Raspberry Chicken with Fresh Raspberries, and Buttermilk Mashed Potatoes

> ½ cup Raspberry vinegar
>
> 2 Tablespoons Dijon mustard
>
> 1 Tablespoon extra-virgin olive oil
>
> ¼ teaspoon white pepper

Thighs Swimming in a Higher State of Garlic Consciousness

This is a simple baked chicken recipe that originated with the legendary American chef James Beard many years ago. I've probably altered it unknowingly, but believe me, if you follow this recipe your mouth will achieve a new level of oral pleasure. Hers will be similarly stimulated.

Dialogue will undoubtedly ensue.

Raw Materials

8-10 good sized thighs

1 15-ounce can of 99% fat-free chicken broth

2 stalks of celery (chopped)

1 medium white or yellow onion (chopped)

1 Tablespoon dried tarragon

Two or three full heads of garlic (outer shell removed, cloves separated but not peeled)

Black Java pepper to taste

1 recipe of steamed white or brown rice

Tools

glass baking dish

knife

cutting board

large pot for rice

Dialogic Chicken

The Blueprint

1. Preheat oven to 325.

2. Cover the bottom of a glass baking dish with chopped celery and onion.

3. Arrange the thighs atop the veggies.

4. Pour the chicken broth over them.

5. Tuck the garlic cloves beneath—and around—each piece of chicken and anywhere else in the baking dish that looks good.

6. Sprinkle the tarragon and black pepper evenly over the top.

7. Cover tightly with aluminum foil and bake at 325 degrees for 2 hours.

8. About 30 minutes prior to done, begin preparing the steamed white rice (50 minutes for brown rice). Follow the package directions. Enough said?

9. Remove the chicken from the oven. Carefully remove the cover from the dish. Breathe deeply; the aroma is unbelievably rich and wonderful. Chances are your nose will have now attained nirvana and your mouth will be watering. These are good signs.

Arrange two or three thighs, a large spoonful of celery and onions, and several pieces of garlic per plate over steamed white rice. Add some of the remaining broth to moisten the rice. Serve immediately with thin slices of sourdough or French bread.

At the table, squeeze the contents of one garlic clove on each slice of the bread. This dish is best with a good quality Beaujolais, White Zinfandel, or an oaky Chardonnay.

Southern Baptist Fried Chicken

I couldn't end this chapter without teaching you how to properly fry a chicken, Southern-style. I learned this method from attending (as a guest) several Southern Baptist dinners, and talking to the women about their secrets of chicken success. I call it Southern Baptist Fried Chicken for this reason, and also because with enough red pepper in it, you can find yourself filled with irreverent chicken temptation that leads rather directly to a hotness that is as firey as a Baptist version of hell.

Frankly, I love to eat spicy fried chicken, even though it means my mouth will require some serious redemption and my body will require a couple of extra hours in the gym the next day. But so what? A guy has to be willing to sacrifice some time, some pain, some effort, for what he loves.

Raw Material

1 whole chicken, cut-up (note: you can use boneless chicken breasts and thighs, or any combination of breasts, thighs, and legs, if you'd rather)

2 cups buttermilk

2 cups all-purpose white flour

1 cup Crisco

1 ½ Tablespoons dried oregano

1 ½ Tablespoons dried basil

1 ½ Tablespoons sweet paprika

½ - 1 ½ teaspoons cayenne pepper (start with a lesser amount, build up to sinful levels slowly)

Sea salt and black Java pepper to taste

Dialogic Chicken

Tools

deep fryer or deep frying pan

large bowl

small bowl

big platter

large plastic bag

cutting board

The Blueprint

1. Wash the chicken pieces; remove excess fat. If you are really concerned about fat, just get rid of all of it.

2. Soak the chicken pieces in the buttermilk for at least 2 hours, or refrigerate overnight.

3. Place the flour on a big platter, in a large plastic bag, or on top of a large cutting board.

4. In a small bowl, blend thoroughly 1 tablespoon of the oregano, 1 tablespoon of the basil, and 1 tablespoon of the paprika.

5. Add this mixture to the flour and run a fork through it (or, if you are using a plastic bag, shake it) several times.

6. Shake excess buttermilk from the chicken pieces.

7. By hand, coat each chicken piece evenly and completely with the remaining seasoning mixture (and *all* of the red cayenne pepper).

8. Dip quickly into the buttermilk. Then coat the chicken pieces in the seasoned flour mixture.

9. Heat the Crisco on medium-high in a large skillet deep enough to accommodate the chicken pieces. If this isn't possible, use two skillets or fry the chicken in batches.

10. Add the chicken to the hot oil and brown each side quickly.

11. Cover the skillet and reduce the heat to low. You want to keep the oil in a constant, but light, state of being bubbly, but not so hot as to burn the chicken before the dark meat is cooked thoroughly.

12. Keep checking the chicken and turning the pieces, recovering the skillet each time. Do this for about 10-12 minutes.

13. Remove the cover, turn up the heat to medium-high, and finish browning for a final 3-5 minutes. Make sure each piece is completely cooked by inserting a fork and seeing if the fluid runs clear. When it does, it's done. Do not overcook or undercook this chicken!

Serve hot or cold with candied yams (sweet potatoes) and green onion potato salad. I like a cold glass of milk with this dish, but have been known to accompany it with beer. Yum!

Candied Sweet Potatoes

You really have to work hard to mess up this dish. Just follow these instructions and you will have perfect sweet potatoes every time.

Raw Materials

4 good-sized sweet potatoes (washed and peeled; cut into 1/4" pieces: cubes, slices, oddly-shaped units, whatever you want to see on your plate)

Nonstick vegetable cooking spray

Dialogic Chicken

1 stick unsalted butter (chopped into pieces)

1 cup dark brown sugar

1 Tablespoon ground cinnamon

1 teaspoon nutmeg

Tools

large baking dish

knife

cutting board

The Blueprint

1. Preheat oven to 350 degrees.

2. Wash, peel, and cut the potatoes.

3. Lightly coat the bottom and sides of a large baking dish with the vegetable spray.

4. Toss in the sweet potatoes and the butter.

5. Sprinkle the whole thing with the brown sugar, the cinnamon, and the nutmeg.

6. Place in the oven.

7. Bake, uncovered, for 45-60 minutes, testing with a fork to see when the desired level of doneness is achieved.

Delightful Diana's Yankee Momma's Variation

Add 2-3 thinly sliced apples and a handful of raisins to the mixture. When the desired level of doneness is achieved, remove from oven and cover the whole thing with a bunch of small marshmallows. Turn the dial on your stove from "bake" to "broil." Place the dish back into the oven under the broiler for 5-10 *seconds*, or until the marshmallows are golden brown. DO NOT WALK AWAY! The marshmallows require almost no time at all to melt, and if they do melt, this otherwise fine dish will become a messy, gooey, sticky, burnt pile of a foodstuff that thoroughly deserves the moniker: Yuk. Probably your dog would even be turned off to it. But done properly, this variation makes for a sweet and aromatic dish that is part veggie side dish and part dessert.

Green Onion Potato Salad

This potato salad has a distinctive Cajun flavor that goes very well with Southern Baptist Fried Chicken and Candied Sweet Potatoes. The original, inspired version was created by none other than the Great Cajun chef Paul Prudhomme; I've taken some small liberties with it to reduce the complexity of the preparation. You'll like it, green onions and all.

 Raw Materials

4-6 Yukon Gold or Russet potatoes (washed and peeled; chopped into bite-size squares)

1 cup Mayonnaise

6 eggs (hard boiled; peeled, and sliced)

4 green onions (washed and finely diced)

1 medium green pepper (finely chopped)

1 medium red pepper (finely chopped)

Dialogic Chicken

2-3 stalks celery (thinly sliced)

1 teaspoon white pepper

1 teaspoon black pepper

1 teaspoon dried mustard

½ teaspoon red cayenne pepper

½ teaspoon paprika

Some sprigs of fresh parsley

Sea salt to taste

(optional): 7 ounce jar of sweet pickle relish

Tools

large pot

small pot

large bowl

knife

cutting board

The Blueprint

1. Place the potatoes in a large pot and cover with cold water.

2. Cook the potatoes over medium-high heat for 10-12 minutes, or until desired level of tenderness is achieved.

3. Pour off the water and cool for half an hour (note: you can speed up the cooling process by placing the pot in your refrigerator for 10-15 minutes).

4. Place the eggs into a small pot, cover with cold water, and boil for 15 minutes.

5. Pour off the water and peel the eggs. Slice.

6. While you waiting for the potatoes to cool and the eggs to boil, mix the spices into the mayonnaise.

7. Chop the veggies.

8. Mix everything together in a large bowl. If you are adding the pickle relish, do it now.

9. Sprinkle a little paprika over the top. Add some fresh sprigs of parsley.

Dr. J.'s Summer Casanova Chicken Salad

Dr. Elizabeth J. Natalle (Dr. J) prepares this intriguing combination of ingredients and serves it when the thick heat of a Carolina summer calls forth the need for a cool dialogic dinner at home. Dr. J. is an intimate communication teacher and scholar; this particular recipe no doubt emerged from years of careful research. You, my aspiring Casanova, will indeed be grateful for its sensuous gifts.

Raw Materials

1 lb boneless chicken breast (washed and trimmed of all fat)

4 ounces frozen sugar snap peas

½ pint of cherry tomatoes

3-4 medium red-skinned potatoes (washed but not skinned)

handful of black olives (Kalamata or Greek)

½- ¾ cup Newman's Own Salad Dressing
        (or Dr. Bud's Balsamic Vinaigrette)

Dialogic Chicken

Sea salt and black Java pepper to taste

(optional) 1 Tablespoon capers

(optional) crumbled Feta cheese to taste

Tools

baking dish

large pot

knife

cutting board

large serving bowl

The Blueprint

1. Preheat oven to 350 degrees.

2. Place washed and trimmed breasts on a pyrex baking dish that you have sprayed lightly with vegetable or olive oil.

3. Place dish on the center rack in your oven.

4. Bake for 20 minutes, or until done.

5. Remove from oven and cut into small, bite-sized pieces.

6. While you are waiting for the chicken to cook, place the potatoes in a medium-sized pot and cover with cold water.

7. Bring to a boil, lower heat to simmer, allow to cook for 10-12 minutes.

8. Remove from stove, drain, run a little cold water over them, allow to cool at room temperature (or place in the refrigerator for 10-15 minutes).

9. Open the frozen box of sugar snap peas. Probably this is an 8-ounce box, so you only need half of these green wonders. Unfortunately, they will all be stuck together.

10. Place in a colander and run cold water over them until they break up, about 2-3 minutes. Separate the half you need from the half you don't. Save the half you don't plan to use. Or double the recipe and make a lot of this salad.

11. Place the diced chicken, cool potatoes, sugar snaps, and tomatoes in a large bowl.

12. Add a dash of salt and pepper.

13, Add olives.

14. Toss with Newman's Salad Dressing (or Dr. Bud's Balsamic Vinaigrette).

15. Add the capers and crumbled feta cheese, if you want to add a little zing.

Serve over cool mesculin greens. Provide extra salad dressing at the table. Dr. J. recommends adding a few nasturtiums as garnish. These are tiny little yellow flowers. Yes, they are edible. No, they aren't aphrodisiacs. But she recommends them, and she is an intimate communication scholar. Savor the mystery . . . tell a story of your own.

Doing Dialogue at Dinner

Dialogue is a good word that has fallen on bad times lately.

As with its historic predecessor "communication," "dialogue" is too often used as a cover-up, as a verbal Band-Aid where serious emergency room stitching is needed. For instance, how many times have you heard "we need a dialogue" coming out of the mouth of a relational partner who you know really means, "I have a list of non-negotiable demands"? Or worse, those people in the workplace who affect a level of false sincerity accented by the tiresome phrase "we need to dialogue." *To* dialogue? Is this the cultural equivalent of "*do*ing lunch?"

The cultural downsizing of this once-great idea is truly unfortunate. Martin Buber, a philosopher/theologian and easily one of the best writers on dialogue, used the idea to pronounce the terms of what he calls the "I-Thou" relationship. Dialogue is both an attitude of respect, humility, and genuine love as well as a way of speaking from the center of that attitude. It is to treat your partner as *sacred*. It is to treat words that pass between you as sacred and yet incomplete vessels of your mutual search for identity and meaning in the universe.

Pretty weighty stuff. Certainly weightier than the pap that it too often refers to today.

Dinner is a wonderful time for dialogue. For real dialogue. Good food inspires it. So does good wine. And if you are a guy who has prepared a veritable feast for his loved one, the gift of a meal can be the setting of an appropriate stage for good talk. It is an offering of love.

Now, as I have pointed out, a chicken is a pretty basic creature, ugly to look at and awkward when it comes to even barnyard social graces. This analogy works as well to describe basic talk. You may recall my diatribe against "phatic communion" in the sandwich chapter; "phatic communion"—merely getting through what is supposed to pass for conversation with cliches and pat phrases—is what I mean by "basic talk." It is what communication theorists call "ritualized utterances." It is a waste of time, a major waste of *our* time *together*.

How many times have you gone out for dinner and witnessed a supposed couple silently eating their meal? Kind of sad, isn't it? They are, as the rock songwriter Dave Mason used to say, "alone together." By contrast, there is always at least one couple in the room who seem to have great energy, who are really enjoying themselves. How do you know this? Because they are speaking to, and listening to, each other. They are using the occasion of dinner to further the interests of their romance, their relationship, their quest.

It would be nice if I could point out, with appropriate empirical support, that they are always dining on chicken. But clearly this would be untrue. Fact is, a couple who has discovered the pleasures of dialogue can do it anytime, anywhere, eating or drinking anything. They can dialogue dressed up, dressed down, or just plain naked. For those couples who have yet to embark on such mutuality, however, chicken works just fine.

Chicken is transformative, remember?

That ugly little non-duckling, plucked and processed, can be marinated and cooked into a higher state of consciousness. So, too, can your exchange of basic talk.

HERE LITTLE PIGGY

"I was cooking some ribs one evening an drinking a
beer, taking life easy on a Saturday afternoon. The ribs
were boiling in some water, getting tender, and about
dark I was going to put them over a fire on grill, slap
some barbecue sauce on them, cook my family a little
feast.... I usually have several cold beers while I am
doing that. The ribs were going to cook for a couple of
hours and I had plenty of beer."

—Larry Brown, <u>On Fire</u>

The Story of the Wolf's Attraction to Pork

Once upon a time there was a big, bad, wolf. Handsome guy, though. Sharp. Had some potential. Loved to eat but didn't know how to cook.

Really loved pork.

He got deeply involved with a lovely sheep, but that relationship just didn't work out. They just couldn't communicate. The sheep ended up totally sheared. The wolf carried around some woolly memories.

Because he was deeply hurt and blamed the whole thing on her, he started believing what his friends told him about members of the opposite breed. You know, infamous old wolves' tale that says "sheep only treat you well if you treat them badly." Big mistake. He tried to treat other sheep badly and they quickly baaahed out of the relationship. This was the 90s, after all. They knew, only too well, that the proverbial forest was full of big, bad, wolves.

By now he had a reputation for being, well, a big, bad, wolf.

And he still couldn't cook. Nor could he communicate.

And he craved, even more than ever, pork.

So what was he to do?

One day he learned that three little pigs had moved into the neighboring village. He was beside himself. *Three* little pigs? Were they cute? Were they well-developed? Had they heard about him yet? He was thinking, no, rather, he was dreaming: PORK.

Turns out, they had. They knew all about his big bad wolfishness. His inability to communicate. His lack of cooking skills.

So they did what any self-respecting set of three pigs would do. They built their own houses, they minded their own business, they planted gardens, and they made friends with just about everyone in the village except Mr. Wolf.

Here Little Piggy

Well, you know part of what happened next. The part where he huffs and puffs and blows down two of the three little pigs houses. Guys who can't communicate often behave this way. And probably you know what happened next. The third little pig, whom had wisely constructed his domain out of brick, successfully defended her sisters and wore out the big, bad, blowhard.

Probably you think that was the end of the story. *Not*!

For you see, the third little piggy understood the wolf's problem. And she saw that he did, indeed, have potential. She knew, in her little pig's heart of hearts, that he could change. He could evolve. He could learn to cook and communicate.

She believed in him. She believed in him so much that one evening she invited him over for dinner. He came, but he wasn't thinking about what was on the stove, if you get my drift. He was, after all, merely a wolf in dinner clothes.

Once inside her house he began to revert to his wolfish ways. "Here little piggy," he cooed. "Come closer. Let me smell your sweet perfume."

She sighed. Maybe this was a lost cause after all. "No," she replied. "Why don't you give me a hand with dinner?"

Now he was a wolf, but he didn't want to appear stupid. He cautiously entered her kitchen. "Okay," he said slowly, "what would you like me to do?"

"You have a choice," she replied. "You can eat me, which is obviously what you came here to do. You will be very happy for one night but will have lost the chance for a real relationship forever. Your reputation will continue to suffer. My sisters have already alerted the sheriff. If you abuse me in any way, your sorry ass will be brought to trial. Your whole sordid relational life will be made public. Chances are good that you will lose your tail. Books will be written making fun of you. You will, forever, be regarded as symbol of failed manhood."

"What's the other choice?" he asked, sorrowfully.

"You can accept this gift from me, a wonderful new cookbook by The Grand Saucier of Southern Simmer and The Reigning Cook-King of Passion, Dr. Bud."

He looked very confused. "Huh?"

"You see, Wolfy," she smiled, "you don't have to go out hunting sheep or blowing down the houses of any little pigs anymore. You can lighten up! Develop a sense of humor. Learn to cook for me—for us—at home. There are four marvelous tenderloin recipes that I'm sure you'll love. And throughout the book you will tips to teach wolves how to really communicate with members of my gender." She sighed. "You can become the man you always wanted to be. We can have fun together. And we can have a *great* relationship."

He thought about it. "You mean I can learn to give members of the opposite breed what they really want?'

"Yes, that's right."

"So what do I get in return?"

"What *you* really want," she said.

And that was all she had to say. It was a done deal.

THE END

Here Little Piggy

All of us wolves know it. Pork is *good*. Pork is *fine*. Pork is the "other" white meat, which means it is generally healthy, but even if it weren't, it wouldn't matter. Pig is too good to miss. In this way, pig is the other red meat too.

In America, pork is deeply symbolic. Many Americans celebrate holidays with either a baked ham or pork roast. Cookouts feature pork ribs, pork chops, or pork barbecue. Eating well on the run means a big ol' ham sam'ich on rye. Eating pig is a sign of doing well, of living off the fat, of being able to enjoy one of the finer meats in life. To "pig out" is truly to feast.

Probably the whole reason for the existence of mustard is the hog.

If it's not, it should be.

Men I know often say that serving pork to a woman is bad idea. Maybe it's the symbolism, because it certainly can't be the taste. Whenever I hear such a thing, I say something properly eccentric, maybe Darwinian, like "evolution works in both sexes and with all genders." Some men get it. Other's don't. It's the ones who don't that you just can't worry about. They don't get it and probably never will.

If that sounds harsh, so be it. I'm not always an angel.

And neither are you.

We are talking *pig* here. Pigs bring out the true hoggliness in me. Succulent, tender, with the same basic consistency as a good steak, flavor that is great just roasting in its own pan juices but that can also be easily enhanced with simple-to-assemble marinades . . . eating pig has nothing to do with symbolism for me. It has everything to do with *taste*. With flavor. With enjoyment.

Women do not always see pork in this light, however.

But I swear it: women who initially object to eating pork can be quietly educated.

Avoid the frontal assault. When pork is the issue, bald assertiveness and plays of Western logic only tend to reinforce our wolfishness. The likely replies are: "So what if it is the 'other white meat?'" and/or "I don't care if *other* women in your life have eaten it." Or this one, the death knoll of pleasure this particular evening: "You can eat it if you have to; I'll make a small salad for myself."

Guys, we are fighting against a *symbolic* world, not an empirical one. We have to use a softer, gentler, more seductive and less deductive approach. Like marketers, we need to associate the consumption of pork with other positive symbols. You can appeal to myth: "Did you know that Venus herself was said to have dined almost exclusively on mesquite-grilled pork tender-loin?" It's an obvious inaccuracy, but the cuteness of it may win some favor. Or you can create a collage of representational patterns that transform the idea of eating pig into something more symbolically palatable: Beauty, truth, lifelong love, endless passion, good wine, great music, lots of money . . . and a Virginia baked ham, that's the ticket!"

Well, you can *try*.

Women often give points for effort. Even failed effort. Sometimes they even give more points for failure.

Such is part of their mystery.

My approach is simpler, less symbolic, and has the added benefit of usually working.

What I do is prepare the following meal.

The proof of the pig is in the eating.

Here Little Piggy

Singularly Great Pork Chops with Lemon Rice and Steamed Spinach

What more can I say?

Raw Materials

2 1" thick butterfly pork chops

2 Tablespoons Balsamic vinegar

2 Tablespoons olive oil

2 cloves garlic (peeled and pressed)

Black Java pepper to taste

1 cup of white rice

1 cup of dry white wine

1 cup of water

Juice of one lemon (squeezed)

Dash of lemon pepper

1 package fresh spinach (washed and de-stemmed)

Enough water for steaming

Tools

grill

large shallow dish

2 large pots or 1 large pot and 1 steamer

serving dishes

spatula or slotted spoon

1. Assemble the marinade by combining the vinegar, oil, garlic and pepper.

2. Place the chops in the marinade, turn once to coat evenly, cover, and refrigerate for 2-3 hours, or overnight.

3. Turn on the gas grill or start the briquettes.

4. Bring the wine and water to a boil for the white rice.

5. Add the rice and the dash of lemon pepper. Cover tightly and cook for 15 minutes.

6. Open the pot and add the freshly squeezed lemon juice, stir three or four times. Cover the pot and turn off the heat.

7. Grill the chops for 4-5 minutes per side. Place them in the microwave for warm safekeeping.

8. Bring the water to boil in the other large pot or steamer.

9. Add the spinach, cover, and steam for about 30 seconds.

10. Open the pot and stir. Cover the pot and steam for an additional 15 seconds. Open the pot and stir again. Chances are good your spinach will be properly steamed.

11. Remove immediately. Using a spatula or large slotted spoon, squeeze the water out of the spinach.

Serve this dish with a salad and a crusty herb bread, roughly cut. I like a good Merlot or Chardonnay with it.

Pork Tenderloin with Veggies in a Crock Pot

As I pointed out in the Dialogic Chicken chapter, a crock pot is a good investment for anyone. For about $30-50, depending on the size of the pot selected, you can enjoy years of excellent meals that cook while you are at work. I've cooked chicken, beef, pork, and vegetable dishes in mine, and with a few spices and a little imagination you can always make productive use of whatever you have on hand. The newer models are also easier to clean because the porcelain crock can be removed from the surrounding metal container.

Here is a simple pork tenderloin recipe that takes about five minutes to prepare.

Raw Material

1 1½ - 2 lb pork tenderloin

1 large onion (Vidalia, if available; peeled and thinly sliced)

2-3 stalks of celery (washed and chopped)

3-4 Russet potatoes (peeled and cut into either slices or chunks)

3-4 carrots or 10-12 baby carrots (washed, peeled, and cut into bit size pieces)

Sea salt and black Java pepper to taste

Tools

crockpot

knife

cutting board

1. Place the onions and celery in the bottom of the crock pot.

2. Place the tenderloin on top of the onions and celery.

3. Sprinkle some pepper over the pork.

4. Add the remaining veggies, cover the crock pot, turn the heat on low.

In 7-9 hours you will have dinner. It is practically impossible to overcook anything in a crock pot. You can leave this roast on low for 10-12 hours and still expect a fine meal.

Three Wonderful Alternatives

If the above basic recipe sounds too bland for your spicy tastes, here are three easy-to-prepare and delicious alternatives.

The Penn State Special

Prepare the dish the same basic way, but omit the potatoes and carrots. About 2 hours prior to serving, uncover the pot and cover the roast with a large package (not can!) of good quality of sauerkraut. Make basic mashed potatoes. Warm up some green peas. Serve the roast with the kraut , add the peas and mashed potatoes as side dishes. If you are true Penn Stater, you will mix the kraut with the mashed potatoes. Serve with a good quality German dark beer.

eryᵒ

California Tenderloin Teriyaki

Try slathering the tenderloin in a commercially-available Teriyaki sauce prior to lowering into the crock. Instead of potatoes, use canned bamboo shoots, mushrooms, and water chestnuts. Serve with a good quality California Reisling or plum wine.

Mexican-Style Carnitas

Pepper the tenderloin with 1 tablespoon (more or less to taste) of ground Ancho chili or chili caribe (those red pepper flakes used on pizza). Omit the chicken broth, potatoes, and carrots. Add 1 cup of water, 1 teaspoon Kosher salt, 2-3 cloves of garlic (chopped), 1 teaspoon anise seed, 2 teaspoons cumin seed, 1 stick of cinnamon, and 2 teaspoons Mexican oregano. Cook for 7-9 hours. Serve with warm tortillas, refried or black beans, sour cream, and salsa. Serve with a good quality Mexican lager.

Tender, Moist, Wonderful Ribs with Fresh Corn on the Cob

A man should be able to cook good ribs. Most men cannot. Most men cover up this failure by either (a) claiming they know a place just outside of town that does ribs better than anything they could do (often this is true), or by (b) covering the ribs with some commercially-produced sauce that dominates the meat because the meat itself has been cooked bone dry.

Face it, ribs are *not* easy to do well. They are incredibly easy to do poorly. And there is no barbecue sauce that can make up the difference.

In the continuing struggle to do what a man has to be able to do—cook ribs—many well-intentioned and sly Southern men I know have invested in a device called "the smoker." Essentially this is a grill with a tight-fitting lid that cooks the meat at a very low temperature for a long, long time.

Smokers are a good idea if you have a lot of time on your hands and know how to use one; otherwise they don't so much as cook the meat as tease-heat to long, lingering death, imparting somewhere in the alledged cooking process a kind of warm-watery-laced-with-hickory flavor that fails to impress anyone. But because the process has taken all night and part of another day, and because saving face is important in relationships, everyone who is forced to "try it" will claim that it is "um-um good." Bull. It still tastes like water and salt to me.

A second option is the Hawaiian method. Dig a big pit in your backyard, prepare a wood fire, toss in a whole pig (dead, of course), light a big fire, cover it with banana leaves, and get very drunk on those sweet rum drinks with the little umbrellas. You'll pass out, of course, the pig will eventually cook, and if you've had enough foresight to invite all of your neighbors, by the time you are nursing a bad hangover the party will have started and the police won't have come. You really can bake a great pig this way, but you leave quite a large, black hole in your yard. Not good for property values.

The third option is to do it my way. It's simple, it's relatively quick, and you can do it at home. Like this:

 Raw Materials

Couple or three-to-five pounds of pork ribs

A little water for steaming

Dale's sauce, or some other commercially-available barbecue sauce of your choice

Couple or four ears of fresh corn on the cob

Black Java Pepper to taste

Here Little Piggy

Tools

grill

baking dish

basting brush

The Blueprint

Ribs require using two sequential methods of cooking: slow roasting in the oven for a long time and grilling over hot coals for a shorter period of time. Begin with slow-roasting.

1. Heat your oven to 250-degrees and place the ribs in a deep glass baking dish.

2. Add enough water to prevent the ribs from sticking to the dish, or about ½ cup.

3. Shake some pepper over the ribs.

4. Cover tightly and roast for two hours.

5. Check the meat about half way through to make sure there is still enough water in the dish to keep the ribs moist. If not, add ¼ - ½ cup of *warm* water. The meat should be mostly cooked by the time you transfer it to the grill. Grilling the ribs is mostly for looks and that essential fire-basted flavor.

6. Slather the ribs with Dale's sauce just prior to grilling. Grill on medium for about 3 minutes per side.

Serve the ribs with the corn and green salad, picnic style. Drink cold beer, iced tea, or Coca-Cola with it. If you are partial to wine, I'd go with a Blush Zinfadel or perhaps a White Vouvray.

On Cooking Corn

About the time you are checking the dish in the oven to see if there is still enough water, you are about ready to decide whether to roast or steam the ears of corn. If you choose to roast them, leave the husks on. If you plan to steam, remove them.

Two Roasting Methods: If you plan to roast the ears in your oven, heat it to 325-degrees, soak the ears in cold water until the desired oven temperature is reached, and then place the ears on the middle rack. In twenty minutes the husks will be brown and the corn will be done. Remove from the oven (use oven mitts!) and serve with softened butter and salt.

NOTE: This method will be hard to manage unless you have two ovens, because the ribs will also be slow-roasting in there. If you want roasted ears but only have one oven, then I suggest firing up your trusty gas grill. Leave the husks on, soak in cold water for five minutes, and roast over low fire for 20 minutes, turning occasionally.

One Steaming Method: Steaming the corn is easier and quicker. Place about 1 cup of cold water in a big pot with a steaming rack along the bottom. Shuck the ears, wash them, make sure you get rid of those pesky little strands of corn hair that, if not properly removed get stuck between your teeth, and place the ears on a steaming rack in the big pot on the stove.

If you don't have a steaming rack, stand the ears on their narrower ends around the circumference of the pot and then lean them inward so the fatter ends touch, making a sort of corn teepee. Add 1 cup of water. Cover the pot. Bring the water to a rolling boil, then turn off the heat. Let the corn slow cook for five minutes. Serve with softened butter and salt. Contrary to popular belief, do *not* put sugar in the water because it only toughens the kernels of corn. If you want sweet corn, then buy the corn that is labeled "sweet corn."

A Honey of a Ham

You can bake a perfectly good ham in your oven at home, or you can purchase any one of a number of honey-baked hams from your local supermarket or brand-name ham specialty store. Frankly, I usually just buy one already cooked. I even buy one that is already sliced—"spiral-sliced."

Really now, you don't believe that everyone who writes a cookbook makes everything from scratch, do you? I'll give you that. But I'm a guy, and I've got to tell the truth to my fellow men. Hence, I offer no baked ham recipe in this cookbook. Sometimes a guy just has to admit that some things are better left to specialists.

So, if you want to serve a honey of a ham, please select the one of your choice and follow the package instructions for reheating it. Or just carve it cold. Offer an assortment of mustards—Dijon-style, honey mustard, sweet mustard, etc., and a stack of sliced rye and/or pumpernickel breads.

Side dishes for a ham dinner are meant to enhance the presence and goodness of the meat, not detract from it. For this reason, I usually stick with the basics: steamed green beans, potato salad, a baked onion. Nothing too fancy.

Ham makes for a wonderful meal or a great sandwich, but it is not meat to be taken very seriously. Think about where it came from, what specific part of the pig you are chowing down on. And for this reason, always remember that ham, like all pig dishes, is best served with a sense of humor.

Developing a Sense of Humor

Good relationships *require* humor to survive. Intimate relationships depend on it.

It is important to understand what I mean by "humor."

I do not mean the ability to tell a joke. Although, this is helpful.

I do not mean to be perpetually happy and jovial. This is unlikely.

And I do not mean that you treat every issue as if it were a page from the comics or an excuse for a one-liner. This is annoying.

What I do mean by "humor" is that you recognize and live with a personal and social sense of fallibility. We are *human*, after all, and humans have perhaps best described by the philosopher/analyst Ernest Becker as "angels with assholes." Another wise man with a keen sense of the rhetorical, Kenneth Burke, after a lifetime of investigating how we use and abuse symbols when we communicate, explained that the only thing that could save the human race was a sense of humor. Without it, we end up taking ourselves, and our circumstances, too seriously. And too much seriousness tends to lead, in affairs of state and affairs of the heart, to war.

Think of it this way. Life is all about making choices. It can be lived as if it is a great tragedy or a good comedy. I know men and women who don't seem to understand this choice, and thereby are condemned to live in the gray in-between netherworld, making themselves and others around them alternately concerned or frustrated. Having mastered the middle ground they fail at being truly happy or at allowing themselves to be truly sad. They may miss the agony, but they also miss the ecstasy. They live under-fulfilled, and therefore stressed, in both directions. And this is too bad because it is entirely avoidable.

Here Little Piggy

Developing a sense of humor does not make you a frivolous person. It does make you healthier, more resilient. It allows you to relieve stress for yourself, and with others. A sense of humor can save you from bad situations, provide you with a much needed belly laugh in those times when nothing else will do.

Nor does developing a sense of humor brand you as unintelligent. By contrast, it requires intelligence to pull off a good sense of humor because you must always be alert to the comic possibilities in the everyday. Kofi Annan, the Secretary-General of the United Nations, said it best when asked by Larry King what he attributed his success in negotiating peace agreements to. His response: "I try not to take myself too seriously."

How does he do that? How should you do that?

A sense of humor is largely derived from two skills. First, as Annan says, to avoid taking yourself too seriously. Second, it is largely crafted by an ability to have fun with words. The first skill is a sign of character and intelligence, the second one is a sign of creativity and joy in life.

I've never met a worthwhile woman who didn't possess a keen sense of humor. Nor have I ever known of a worthwhile woman who didn't believe that her man must have one, too. Women like men who can make them laugh, and who can help keep them happy.

Cooking is a way of seeing and understanding that. Following any recipe is like following the path or journey of your life. You can read all the instructions and still, once in a while, just get it wrong! When this happens, you have a choice. You can laugh, or you can cry. Nobody likes a crybaby. And crybabies don't seem to have the right stuff to try again.

But those of us who laugh in times of trouble are the ones we most admire, respect, and want to hang around with. By being able to turn the bad situation around with a humorous word or deed, those who can laugh change our perspective. Those who laugh teach us to see the situation differently. Those who laugh re-create it in a better light.

No wonder this is the sort of man any real woman wants around.

Someone she can share pig with.

So, my friend, lighten up!

A sense of humor and good intimate relations go hand in hand.

SEAFOOD IS THE BEACH

"She opened the door of her apartment wearing
brief cutoff jeans and a T-shirt imprinted with a large
crimson question mark. No smile. I thought she
looked smashing . . .
She could not resist the stone crabs with mustard
sauce . . . I shall not repeat the details of our
conversation that Sunday afternoon—some things
are sacred. But when the wine was finished (with
enough stone crabs left for a nibble later) she
looked at me intently and asked, 'Have you been
faithful to me, Archy?'

—Lawrence Sanders, <u>McNally's Puzzle</u>

Making a Night Out of Today's Catch

In matters of intimate communication between women and men, the very idea of seafood often works as a rhetorical inducement. The thought of it casts a spell, alerts the senses, promotes a summery vision of all that can be allegorically alluded to in Delbert McClinton's immortal tune: *Sandy Beaches*.

Seafood is deep sorcery for the soul, a way of conjuring the white sands and too-blue seas moved by light breezes; the endless rolling and crashing of moon-swept tides; the imperatives brought forth by the presence of scantily clad, deeply tanned, and adventurous warm bodies; of pure sunshine, gentle afternoon rains, a surround of surf music; of imagined possibilities.

Into this co-joining of the imagination and word magic, the wise man serves a thematically-appropriate dinner. You want to become that wise man, pal. Trust me on this.

Preparing seafood means respecting its origins. Nothing is more fundamental to human life than the rich collaboration of air and the sea, of men and women. Nothing is more natural. In other words, don't mess with it too much!

Keep your preparation *simple*.

Avoid overdoing the fire or prolonging the cooking times.

Don't try to cover up with rich sauces what God has provided and what nature timelessly abides.

Reserve your spice rack and macho inclinations for side dishes and fish stories. In that order.

In this section I provide a practical primer for mostly discriminating men who want to do well with women and seafood. No recipe is difficult. Success is in the finesse.

Seafood is the Beach

Succulent Shrimp

Many men seem to have trouble with the basic idea of foreplay. Without getting too graphic, allow me to describe the problem this way: What's happening on the inside of "the Other" is not as important as what she (er, pardon me, "the Other") looks like, and feels like, on the outside. What these men seem to miss is the concept of slow-building, *internally-generated* heat, particularly when it comes to matters relating to delicate flesh.

So, these guys tend to overcook seafood and make insensitive lovers. Women know this. Guys must learn to respect what is ordinary, everyday, and entirely natural to "the Other." As anthropologists know, learning the everyday lifeways of the native is key to understanding the nature of their differences, as well as to understanding how to communicate effectively with them.

By now my overt analogy ought to be painfully clear. Women and seafood are often seen by men as "different." They represent "the Other." For this reason, a guy who has learned how to grill a steak, or cook a pork chop, or toss a fine pasta, may not necessarily do well with shrimp, salmon, or shark. It is worse when he tries to grill fish or shrimp. However, if such a fellow is willing to learn about the essence of Otherness, chances are good that not only will he improve his seafood techniques, but that in so doing, his understanding of, and ability to perform, in matters of foreplay will also improve.

Well, at least that's the *hope*.

Here's my confession. I'm not very good at confessing, most guys aren't, but here it is. I, too, used to overcook seafood. It was a deficiency of mine, but, hey, I faced it squarely, dealt with it, and overcame it. You can too. I didn't overcome it by myself, however. I needed help. I asked for it. My wife came to my aid. Now I am coming to yours.

Seasoned Shrimp with Baked Potatoes and Country Corn on the Cob

Remember back a couple of chapters, when I said that to truly understand a woman you need to watch what she does for herself, when she is by herself? Same thing is true here. For years my wife would volunteer to "do the shrimp," a fact of our married, culinary life that always mildly surprised me. Usually she was more than happy just to let me cook. But when it came to shrimp, well, she intervened. She was nice about it, but there it was. I just didn't understand.

I didn't have what it takes. I treated shrimp, as they say, without the proper respect. I overcooked it, then apologized. Or I made a big deal of "grilling it," only to serve a tough, moderately blackened dish that didn't make anyone happy; nor did it properly honor Poseidon, the eternal God of the Sea.

So I began watching her, my significant Other, prepare shrimp. I noticed that she did this gently. Using the idea of internally-generated heat. Something that is natural to women, alien to most men. Eventually, I learned from her example.

I am better for the experience. You will be too.

Raw Material

1 lb of large, Gulf-Coast shrimp (rinsed thoroughly, but kept in the shell)

1 can of domestic beer (not dark beer, and never light beer)

1 Tablespoon Old Bay Seafood Seasoning

2 large Russet baking potatoes

Tin foil, enough to cover the potatoes

2 Tablespoons of unsalted butter

Black Java pepper

Seafood is the Beach

2 ears of fresh corn on the cob

Water

Sea salt

(optional) Red Seafood Sauce

 Tools

large pot

medium pot

 The Blueprint

1. Preheat your oven to 450 degrees.

2. Wash the skins of the potatoes thoroughly, and poke a fork into each Russet three times on each side.

3. Rub the skins with softened butter and black pepper, wrap tightly in tin foil, and place on the center rack in the oven.

4. Set the timer for 1 hour.

5. Shuck the corn. Make sure to remove all of those annoying strands of corn hair.

6. Rinse the ears. Place them in enough cold water to cover the ears.

7. When the timer goes off for the potatoes, turn on the heat for the corn. Turn it on *high*.

8. When the water reaches a full boil, turn off the heat, cover, and let stand for five minutes.

9. Set the timer for five minutes so you don't foul up.

10. While you waiting for the corn to finish cooking, turn off the oven. You may leave the potatoes in the oven, or you can remove them.

11. Now prepare the shrimp.

12. Heat the beer in a skillet over a medium flame until it begins to simmer.

13. Mix the Old Bay Seasoning into the beer and bring the fragrant stew back to a low simmer.

14. Toss in the shrimp.

15. Stir gently.

16. Watch for the shrimp to turn bright pink.

17. Immediately turn off the heat.

18. Pour the shrimp into a colander and drain. DO NOT RINSE!

Serve the shrimp with the potato and corn. Place one of those commercially-available red seafood sauces on the table, if you feel like you have to. Maybe some melted butter and lemon wedges. I serve beer with this dish, but a good White Chardonnay is also acceptable.

Other Ways to Use the Shrimp in this Recipe

Now that you have mastered the basic shrimp technique, there are several ways to apply what you have learned.

Option 1: Shrimp Salad

After cooking the shrimp, cool them in the refrigerator (for 20 minutes) or the freezer (for 5 minutes) and then peel. Serve as a topping to any combination of leaves (e.g., spinach, Romaine, green leaf, red leaf, or mixed baby greens). Add Dr. Bud's Basic Vinaigrette or just squirt some fresh lemon juice on it.

Option 2: Shrimp Po' Boy

After cooking the shrimp, cool and peel. Toss with 1 or 2 tablespoons of red seafood sauce, preferably one with some serious horseradish to it. Place a generous amount of this combination in the middle of a halved loaf of fresh, crusty French bread.

Option 3: Cold Shrimp

After cooking the shrimp, cool but don't peel them. Keep covered in the refrigerator until ready to eat. Serve with red seafood sauce and crackers as an appetizer or as a snack.

Grilled Salmon with Mixed Caesar Salad and Brown Rice

Salmon is my favorite summer fish and makes an excellent choice for a simple dinner, particularly when grilled. Now that you have learned the lesson of "internally-generated heat," please remember to apply it here as well.

Some truths are eternal.

Grilling salmon requires almost no preparation and very little talent. What it does require is some olive oil and lemon pepper, a watchful eye, an ability to tell time, and, of course, a grill. If you have these items and talents, then chances are good that you can deliver unto yours a lovely little dinner.

I have included a simple mixed Caesar salad and brown rice as suggested sides, but you are a creative fellow, so do what you like. Rather, do what *she* likes. If your relationship hasn't progressed that far yet, then do it my way. You can't lose. I'm going to make this recipe *very* simple for you.

Raw Material

2 Salmon fillets (about ¼ - 1/3 pound each; you can use the steaks, but they often have bones. Most women don't approve of bones. Well, *those* bones, anyway.)

1 Tablespoon olive oil

½ Tablespoon lemon pepper

¼ pound fresh spinach (washed, destemmed, and ripped into bite-sized pieces)

¼ pound fresh Romaine lettuce (washed, destemmed, and ripped . . .)

¼ cup fresh Parmesan cheese

Some croutons

Dr. Bud's Mock Caesar Dressing (see salads chapter)

1 cup of Uncle Ben's Brown rice (the box that says, clearly, "cooks in 30 minutes")

1 cup of water, and 1 cup of white wine

1 Tablespoon of unsalted butter

Some sea salt, to taste

Tools

grill

glass baking dish

medium pot

Seafood is the Beach

The Blueprint

Begin with what takes the longest time to cook. That would be the *rice*. Follow the instructions on the box. If you can't do that, maybe because you were temporarily seized by a bout of male stupidity and threw the box away, or your large and uncompromising dog ate it, then simply bring the water and white wine to a boil (which is best accomplished over *high* heat), add the butter and rice, stir three or four times, cover tightly, reduce the heat to low, and cook for 30-50 minutes, depending on the kind of rice. Set the timer, don't take unnecessary chances.

Option: Add lightly sautéed (in butter and olive oil) Cremini and/or Portobello mushrooms to the rice.

Then make the salad. If you've already thoroughly rinsed the greens, and ripped the spinach and Romaine leaves into bite-sized pieces, then all you need to do is (a) combine them (artfully, if possible) in a large wooden salad bowl; (b) top with the Parmesan cheese and croutons; and chill (in the fridge) until you are ready to serve. Serve it with the salad dressing at the table. If you are feeling particularly able, pour the dressing over the salad and toss like you've seen done in a restaurant (well, let's modify that: in a restaurant where the salad server knew what he or she was doing).

Now you are ready to prepare the salmon.

1. Place the salmon into a glass baking dish.

2. Brush both sides of the pink surfaces of the fish with Extra Virgin olive oil.

3. Sprinkle with lemon pepper, but avoid overdoing it. A little lemon pepper goes a long way. Keep the salmon in the glass baking dish until you are ready to grill.

4. Prior to heating, coat the cooking surface of the grill with nonstick vegetable oil or spray. This will prevent the salmon from sticking, thereby losing its skin and making an ugly presentation. If you don't have vegetable oil spray on hand, pour a little oil onto a paper towel and rub it on the grill. Again, make sure you have coated the grill *before* heating it, or else you are very likely to experience intense pain and have the opportunity to see what your own charred flesh looks like. Remember, you are serving fish, not hands. And make sure the grill is clean first. If it isn't, you are a fool and should not be allowed to have matches, much less relations with a woman.

5. You want the grill to be ready for the salmon when you've got about 15 minutes left on the rice. If you are using a gas grill, allow the cooking surface to heat up thoroughly on high for three minutes.

6. Place the fish on the grill and reduce the heat to "low."

7. Cover and grill for two minutes. Turn the fish and continue cooking for 10 minutes, or until the salmon is no longer dark pink in the middle. You are going for light pink and moist, not white and dry. This sentence will make sense to you if you give it some thought. Remember what you learned in science class: The longer the application of heat, the more moisture is lost. For this very scientific reason, you want to cook the salmon on low heat for *only* 10 minutes. Got it?

Remove the salmon to a serving plate and bring to the table. Retrieve the salad from the refrigerator and the rice from its pan, and serve all of this with a fine wine. Chardonnay is always a good choice, but some people (myself included) prefer a fruity Beaujolais with this dish. Still others, like my sea-going Bulgarian brother-in-law Richard, believe that salmon ought to be served with a vintage Cabernet or Merlot.

Voodoo Catfish with Meuniere Sauce, Smoked Oysters, Shrimp, and Collards

Some women really love spicy food. Especially New Orleans-style spicy food.

I *appreciate* such women. So should you. They know what's good in life.

The dish I am about to teach you to prepare is not for the faint-hearted, or overly-sensitively tongued. Nor is it particularly easy to prepare. But the results are worth the effort and the style of preparation is peculiarly manly. The after-dinner results that are likely to follow from the meal are even more so. So bear with me.

This dish will make you into a different kind of man. Voodoo *does*. Voodoo catfish is *dangerously* delicious!

Raw Materials

2 good-sized catfish fillets (you can also use sea bass, grouper, or red snapper)

1 cup of whole milk (not skim!)

2 eggs

1/4 cup brown mustard

1 1/2 cups of all-purpose white flour (or cornmeal, if you prefer)

1 teaspoon red cayenne pepper

1 teaspoon black Java pepper

1 teaspoon white pepper

1 teaspoon sweet paprika

2 teaspoons garlic powder

2 teaspoons dried oregano

1 teaspoon sea salt

1 teaspoon thyme

1 cup of peanut oil

½ can 99% fat-free chicken broth

2 sticks of unsalted butter (about ½ pound)

1 teaspoon minced garlic

2 Tablespoons flour

¼ cup Worcestershire Sauce

Sea salt to taste

1 tin of smoked oysters (drained)

1 bunch collard greens (washed and torn or sliced into 2" long strips)

2 or 3 strips of uncooked bacon or a fist-sized ham hock (optional)

1 order of steamed succulent shrimp (see above recipe)

Handful of roasted pecans (Use whole pecans; roast on baking sheet for five minutes at 325 degrees)

Tools

medium sauce pan

small sauce pan

2 loaf pans

frying pan

cookie sheet

serving platter

Seafood is the Beach

The Blueprint

Begin by playing some Cajun music. This helps. It's even better if you can sing along. This is voodoo, remember. Begin by preparing the Meuniere Sauce. This is so disgustingly loaded with calories and fat that you should never admit using it to anyone, ever. On the other hand, it is *so* good that if eaten only once in a while, any cost to your health is likely to be fair.

1. Combine the chicken stock and the garlic in a medium-sized saucepan.

2. Bring to boil over high heat, reduce heat to low simmer, and cook for two minutes.

3. Remove the pan from the stove.

4. Melt one stick of the butter in a small pot or saucepan using high heat. When it is bubbly, turn down the heat to low and add the flour.

5. Wisk like you're life depends on it for 10-15 seconds. Remove from heat.

6. Place the stock back on the stove, on medium heat.

7. Add the butter mixture and whisk until smooth and creamy.

8. Reduce the heat to low.

9. Break off chunks of the remaining stick of butter and add to the stock, whisking each time until smooth.

10. Add the Worcestershire sauce slowly, then the sea salt to taste. Allow to cook until thickened a bit, which usually takes 3-5 minutes.

11. Cover the pot and turn off the heat.

12. Prepare the shrimp as per instructions earlier in this chapter. If you have some on hand in the refrigerator, use them.

13. Open the tin of smoked oysters and drain them.

14. Roast the pecans by placing them on a cookie sheet in a 325 degree oven for ten minutes or so. At this point, the combination of aromas in your kitchen will become magical. It's the Voodoo.

15. Now you are ready to cook the collards. Some people like to cook collards for hours at a time, and flavor them with bacon or ham hocks. This is fine if you want to end up with salty, limp greens. And I even like salty limp greens once in a while. *But not with this dish.* What you want to do here is wilt the collard strips, not cook them to death. To wilt the collards, simply place them on a steamer rack over 1 cup of boiling, salted water. If you feel obliged to, you can place two or three strips of uncooked bacon or a ham hock over the greens, but you don't have to. There will be enough flavor in this dish without the added pork. Wilting takes about five minutes, longer if the collards are older, a little less time if you just picked them out in your garden. They will look deep green, a little shriveled but still firm, and that is how you want them to look. When that happens, turn off the heat.

16. To prepare the catfish, assemble two loaf pans.

17. Combine all the seasonings in a small bowl and stir well.

18. In the first pan, place the flour (or cornmeal) and 3 tablespoons of the spices. In the second loaf pan, mix the mustard with the whole milk.

19. Rub the remaining seasoning mix into the fillets. Dip each fillet into the milk and mustard, then into the flour. Coat evenly.

20. Turn the heat on your stove to high, and place the peanut oil in the pan to a depth capable of covering the fillets.

21. Heat until very hot, or until you can drop a dash of the flour mixture into the pan and it sizzles immediately.

22. Place the fillets into the hot oil and *stand back*. The oil will pop and squeak, the fish will begin immediately to cook, and hot oil under these conditions tends to hop out of the skillet, so be careful!

23. Cook each fillet for two minutes on each side and promptly remove from the skillet.

24. Drain on paper towels that you have placed on a large plate.

25. Turn off the heat under the skillet but leave the pan alone. It will be too hot to handle.

Assemble the dinner by placing a little Meuniere Sauce in the middle of each plate, placing a few strips of collards across the whole plate, and laying the fillet in the middle on top of the collards. If the plate is an analog clock face, place the smoked oysters to the right (from noon til 6p.m.) and the shrimp to the left (from 6p.m. til midnight), artfully at hourly intervals. The order is important; this is Voodoo.

Drop more than a little Meuniere Sauce and a few roasted pecans on the top of the fillet, and serve with crusty French bread. I prefer a light white with this dish, a Sauvignon Blanc or Pinot Grigio, for instance. The food is so rich and flavorful that the wine is mostly to cleanse the palate after each bite.

Telling Your Life Story and, More Importantly, Listening to Her's

Relational talk deepens to intimacy with the advent of serious self-disclosure. For most people, this begins by accounting for the journey you life has taken, known colloquially as "telling your story."

Good life stories, ones that you enjoy telling and listening to—regardless of the individual lines in their plots—have a general pattern and some key characteristics. This pattern and the key characteristics are important, because without them, what gets said just isn't a *story*. It just doesn't hang together properly, which, in the communication field (thanks to Dr. Walter Fisher) is known as "lacking narrative fidelity." And you risk being taken for a meandering, self-absorbed, long-winded, chatterbox, which, in the communication field, is known as "being a meandering, self-absorbed, long-winded chatterbox."

Don't let that happen to you.

The proper pattern for story telling is pretty simple. All stories have beginnings, middles, and endings. This means that they start somewhere, and end somewhere, and what happens in between tends to lead the listener to an ending that *feels* like ending when it happens. When this occurs, as if by magic, the beginning *feels* like a beginning, and what happened in between will seem to have *thematically* linked them.

To successfully accomplish this pattern requires thinking about your life as if it were a story, and to see the events and people in your life as helping you to acquire its theme. Your theme should be revealed by your choices of actions in those events and with those people.

Seafood is the Beach

> What emerges from a well-told life story is a clear sense of your identity, as a person, how you understand yourself, and how you've understood the summative meaning of the major events in your life. It is not as important to live an epic existence so much as it is important to make what you have lived through meaningful to yourself and to others.

A lot of men, and women, have trouble with that. They think that no matter what they have lived through, because they, personally, have lived through it, it's *got* to be important. Or, that because it's important to Me, it's got to be important to You. Or, if I just make my face appear like what I am saying is deeply important, it will be. Not true. Unless what you have lived through comes across in a vivid and interesting fashion, and hangs together as a story, the events in your life simply won't matter to anyone short of a sociopath who will be using what you disclose to gain control over you.

You don't want that to happen.

So learn to work on your life story. Think of what you've been through *musically*, as a series of motifs—riffs—that support some kind of general theme. Or perhaps like interdependent chapters in a good novel. When you learn to think about your life as a story, you will find that not everything you've lived through will fit the theme. You can deal with this in two ways. Option #1: You can chalk those up to "learning experiences," and briefly point out how they detracted from your path. Or, Option #2, you can omit them. If they are boring, make sure you select option #2.

There are also some other tactful options. Like when you are asked how many lovers you've had prior to her, you *can* and *should* edit the story of you life.

How do you figure out what the theme of your life is, or has been? Good question. The answer is that nobody can tell you the answer to that. You have to figure it out, alone or with somebody close to you. The important thing is to isolate what communication scholars call *"turning points"* and *"memorable messages"* in your life. These are the times when you either came to a new understanding, or changed a previous one; both of them have made a lot of difference to you.

Another good and proven technique for discovering the pattern and theme of your life story is figuring out what has made you *happy.* Where were you? What were you doing? Who were you with? What was the essence of that moment?

Finally, you can discover your theme by asking what makes you feel that you are living life with *purpose*? Perhaps this sense of purpose connects your life to a broader overall purpose in the Universe. Perhaps it provides you with a motive for your actions. Or perhaps it gives you strength and direction, or even the will to overcome obstacles.

Think of this exercise as a way of connecting the individual dots that have made up your life in order to discover the overall pattern, the theme, what you are here for. Once you have discovered the pattern, you will know your beginning, your middles, and, perhaps, even your end.

> Telling your life story is important, but listening to hers is much more so. Not "just" listening, mind you. But *how* you listen. Where your eyes focus, and remain, during the story. What your face does. Whether or not you interrupt, offer sympathy, or just sit there as if what you are really waiting for is this story to be *over.*

Seafood is the Beach

Listening to someone else's life story should be an exercise in empathy, *not* criticism, and *never* judgment. You want to understand the other person, not evaluate her. You want to gain clues to how she thinks and feels, to her personality, to the values she uses to make decisions.

To do this requires intense listening and an open mind. In many cases, it also requires listening with an open heart. Remember, as Nick Carroway's dad tells him in *The Great Gatsby*, "not everyone has had the advantages you've had," to which we all should add: And nobody has the power to change the past. What you hear may not always be to your liking, but *your* liking isn't necessarily the point.

The point is all about the telling of it. The disclosure of self to another. The place you, as a listener, as a partner, may occupy in the evolving tale.

Life stories are powerful recipes that govern both your understanding and your outcomes. We live within the lines of the stories we tell. We come to know from sharing them. We come together when the lines in those stories finally merge.

And when they do merge, nothing will ever be the same.

MORNINGS ARE FRITTATA

"I did not know how she would be in the morning.

I could only hope that she would not be

bubbly, girlish, and coy."

—John D. MacDonald, <u>The Deep Blue Good-By</u>

"You Say Tomato,"

"I Say Tomata . . ."

"You Say Forever?"

" . . . I Say Frittata!"

There's Got to be a Morning After . . .

The Morning After is always a little scary. Breakfast in bed helps. It allows a groggy man to exit gracefully, spend a little time by himself in the kitchen figuring things out, perhaps trying to remember what he might have said (or promised!), and provides a pleasant way to reenter the bedroom a sure winner. This assumes, of course, that the male in question will have also spent a little time in the bathroom freshening his breath and combing his hair (at least!).

Women, like God, respect cleanliness.

At least the ones you *want* to wake up with do.

While you are preparing breakfast you ought to consider your emotions and your actions from the night before. Recall what happened, honestly. Remember what you said? Yeah, *that.* Chances are very good that she will.

If last night you fully embodied the role of a modern man, a guy who believed, earnestly, in absolutes, who feared no ultimates, who made those clearly articulated and entirely unambiguous promises, well, now is probably *not* the time to suddenly backslide into some form of postmodern ploy: "Well, love is such a complicated ideological position, you know? I'm not sure how I feel about such an obviously hegemonic distortion of meaning for what were, after all, only our mutually-coordinated bodily actions."

You can't say that. Even if you do know what it means.

Mornings are Frittata

Against this kind of low-dog conversation, you can instead bake an omelet, which is known in culinary circles as a "frittata." Rhymes with "tomata." This isn't any ordinary omelet; this is a really *good* omelet. It's chocked full of fresh veggies and a little cheese, and the whole thing is a delight, complex enough for the most discriminating palate yet mild enough for breakfast in bed.

By serving it instead of your postmodern lament, you can direct the initial conversation toward food, which is something both of you can still believe in, enjoy, and talk honestly about. It's always a good beginning. From there, the wise man always allows the woman to "go first" with any declarations of emotion, evaluations of performance, likelihood of a future together, and so on.

Face it, you don't have a real clue about much of anything until then.

So keep it fun.

Keep the conversation light.

Enjoy your breakfast.

The Morning After Frittata

Breakfast in bed is another one of those times, by the way, where, if the talk veers into an unexpected or unwanted direction, having a really good sense of humor is likely to be the only thing capable of saving you. Or, at least your heart. If you really get desperate, ask her how she likes her frittata.

Raw Material

7 medium eggs (NOTE: Always use medium eggs; they are generally from younger hens and definitely have more flavor.)

2 Tablespoons extra virgin olive oil (pardon the irony)

1 thinly-sliced small white or yellow onion (preferably Vidalia)

1 thinly-sliced and then quartered small zucchini

4 or 5 sliced and quartered white mushrooms

8 or 9 green olives, sliced

½ red pepper, thinly sliced

¼ lb grated cheese (Gruyere, white Vermont Cheddar, or whatever you like)

Black Java pepper and sea salt to taste

Tools

large baking dish or glass pie plate

oven mitts

knife

cutting board

The Blueprint

1. Preheat the oven to 450 degrees.

2. Peel the onion and slice it into thin circles.

3. Place the sliced onion in the bottom of an eight or nine inch glass, ovenproof pie plate. Do *not* try to do this with one of those flimsy aluminum pie plates.

4. Pour the olive oil over the onions; make sure the bottom of the pie plate is lightly coated.

5. Place in the oven.

6. Set the timer for five minutes.

7. Return to the cutting board and slice and quarter the rest of the veggies.

8. Break the eggs over a medium-sized bowl and lightly beat with a wire whisk or fork. "Lightly" means just until the yellowness of the stirred yolks achieves oneness with the clear egg-white stuff. If you overbeat it, you'll go blind. Just kidding.

    The truth: if you overbeat your eggs, they won't rise and fluff properly. And I'm not kidding about that. If you've ever made an omelet that turned out thin, flat, and tough, this is probably what you did.

9. When the timer goes off, remove the pie plate from the oven. The oil will be hot and bubbly, and the onions will just have begun to turn light brown.

10. Place the veggies on top of the onions.

11. Sprinkle the cheese over the veggies.

12. Pour the egg mixture over the whole thing.

13. Sprinkle a little sea salt and pepper over the top. DO NOT STIR! The eggs will eventually wrap around the whole pie.

14. Put the whole thing back in the oven and set the timer for 20 minutes.

Go take a shower and shave. When the timer goes off, remove the finished dish. It will be lightly browned on top and the eggy middle of the baked omelet should be just firm. How will you know? Stick a fork in it. If it comes out clean, the frittata is perfect. If you get runny eggy mess on the fork, it's not. If this is the case, turn your oven to "broil" and place the pie plate back in the oven for about 30 seconds to 1 minute, or until it looks firmer and the fork comes out clean. Then remove. Cut into wedges and serve with freshly squeezed orange juice, chilled Champagne, and a single long-stemmed red rose.

Caramelized Bacon

Some women like bacon, some don't. If she does like it, then place six strips of the best pig strips you can buy on that square baking dish you almost used for the omelet. Mix ¼ cup of chopped pecans and 1 tablespoon of brown sugar together in a small bowl and pour the mixture over the bacon. Bake at the same time you put in the omelet, for 20 minutes. Drain on paper towels. You will end up with caramelized bacon that is a sweet and very special treat.

Fresh Fruit

Serving a small bowl of fresh fruit alongside the frittata is always a good idea. The contrast in flavors and textures, the colorful mix of the whole display, what can I say? The whole thing works. This is an especially good idea if you aren't sure what she likes to eat. It gives her a choice, which is a gentlemanly thing to do.

I like to mix a variety of fruits in the bowl. I use green Granny Smith apples, blueberries, strawberries, and bananas. Sometimes I add kiwi or melon. Cherries. Grapes. It's hard to blow this one. Almost any combination is delicious.

The trick is to make the presentation look as good as possible. For this reason, you ought to squeeze the juice of half a lemon or lime over the fruit. Keeps it from turning brown and looking like something you prepared a long time ago.

Toast and Jam

This ought to go without saying, but hey, you are a guy and this is a learning experience, so I won't omit anything. Never serve an omelet naked. Too suggestive. Eggs of any kind always must be served with toast and jam. Use a good quality multi-grained bread (nothing that is wrapped in plastic at the grocery store; go to a bakery!) and a high quality jam. Slice the bread thickly, toast it well.

EXPLOITING HER
WEAKNESS FOR DESSERTS

"'It's amazing that no matter how small women's

bathing suits get, they still manage to cover all

they're supposed to,' I said.

'Do I hear disappointment in your voice?'

Susan said.

'Yes.'"

—Robert B. Parker, <u>Chance</u>

Buy the Dessert . . . But Make the Coffee

Women have a weakness for desserts. It is a deep weakness. Legendary. Even among the strongest of them, this weakness cannot be addressed by any known therapy, nor can it be cured.

It can, however, be exploited. That may sound cold, but listen up. You've come this far, haven't you? Well, *then*. Dessert is *not* an option. Too many otherwise well-intentioned guys have learned the hard way that scrimping on dessert is likely to lead to disappointment. *Your's*. And her's.

Here's why. Dessert is *never* really about food. It is partly about romance, and partly about attitude. But it is mostly about something else that I'll get to in a moment. Think of it this way: Even for the most diet-conscious fitness Nazi feline among us, the whole idea of saying "no" to dessert is somewhere between unseemly and downright impolite. Oh, don't get me wrong. She may, at first, lightly reject the idea. She may, in fact, whisper "no, I just *couldn't*."

What she is really saying is "*beg* me."

Now do you get an inkling about the true meaning of dessert for a woman?

> The main thing to know is that dessert, for a woman, is always about *power* and *control*. It is about the willpower to say "no"; it is about the ability to maintain control over her basic emotion to surrender to the temptation. If you understand these things, you can counter the initial rejection competently.

How? I knew you'd ask. To begin with, you have to appreciate what is at stake here. What you are asking her to do is give up something she has probably sworn—and sworn *repeatedly*—not to give in to. She has made a promise to herself, perhaps even to God, not be tempted by it, not to salivate so readily at the opportunity for it, and never, ever, to eat the whole thing. Especially not on the first date.

By comparison, this would be akin to your most earnest pledge to yourself, and undoubtedly to the porcelain God, not to drink multiple straight shots of tequila on a dare, *ever,* well, at least not on a *week*night.

So to understand what you must do to counter the initial rejection of what has obviously been surrendered to in the past, you need to think about what it would take to get *you* to break such a promise. Then add about 10 times the resistance to that, because women are fundamentally stronger at this than we are.

Would you do it for simple coaxing? Naw. Pleading? Never! Would you do it in exchange for a promise of secrecy? Hmmmmm. Now we are getting somewhere. And would you do it because—on the grand scale of human desire—the anticipation of certain sensual ecstasies outweighs the . . . *calories?*

I thought so.

You see, you just have to think about it from her point of view. Realizing, of course, that she is probably a lot like you are on every level.

Yes, that could be scary. But it is true.

In matters of love and dessert, only the strong know how to properly surrender.

Now it may seem a little crude to suggest, particularly in this day and politically-correct age, that you should exploit a weakness of her's. Particularly in the manner I've just described. But I prefer to frame the issue this way, via 1 Corinthians: "Love suffereth long, and is kind."

Dwell on the meaning of that zen-sounding item for very long and you'll see that what's at stake here is long-term happiness, not a mere short-term giving in. This isn't really about the consumption of calories, or fat, or the decadence that comes so naturally to the lips of one licking off the last smear of rich chocolate from a long, thin finger . . . .

No! This is about seeing how far you will go, without actually saying so.

What we have here is an example of what communication theorists call "analogic discourse." In layman's terms (no pun intended), this means "what we are *really* talking about while we are obstensibly discussing something else entirely." A part of any analogic discourse is its "relational value," which is to say an up-to-the-minute summary judgment of how we feel about "you and me and the bedpost" while tempted by the very presence of anticipatory ecstasy. Dessert is, therefore, merely operating as a metaphor here. In fact, dessert is the thinking man's analogic transition to another room.

"To dessert" is, considered this way, a very transient verb. That is why you don't want to *not* include dessert in your plans for the evening. Without it, you might as well rent a good movie and practice up on your intransient verbs, because this is what you two will likely become.

I don't think I could make it any clearer.

And remember, dessert is something she has to *want* to surrender to . . . .

That having been stated, then, it may seem odd that I've included a chapter on desserts but don't include any recipes.

Here's why. This is a cookbook designed to be used by real men. And real men—even those of you who have mastered the fine art of cooking—are not likely to invest in the equipment, the time, or the expertise required to make really good desserts.

Furthermore, if a guy has prepared one of my dinners, he shouldn't have to. What he should do, instead, is find a really fine bakery in town and purchase whatever looks particularly appealing. I don't mean donuts. I mean something rich and preferably chocolatey; one of those multi-but-thinly layered chocolate cakes with the truffles on top will do nicely. Or, if you are in the mood for something lighter, a fresh fruit tart with fresh whipped cream. A warm (you can still use the oven, right?) berry or apple pie, with a generous scoop of premium Vanilla ice cream.

There are some negatives. Don't do cheesecake. Too cliched. And too fattening.

No brownies, either. This isn't a sixties film.

Best bet: talk to the head baker and get a recommendation based on what you are planning to serve for dinner. Bakers *know.* Believe me.

What you can do is make a fresh pot of coffee. Decaf or regular, flavored, whatever. Buy your own beans and grind them yourself. I buy mine at the Carolina Coffee shop in Greensboro, North Carolina. If you are using one of those flavored varieties (or even if you aren't), you can add a couple of teaspoons of sugar to the grounds to sweeten the deal. If she doesn't drink it, fine. The aroma is still worth it.

Offer her an after-dinner drink. If she doesn't go for that either, then ask her what she *is* in the mood for . . . as you slowly, gently, reach over to remove the last little bit of chocolate from her lips.

Desserts are never really endings, now are they?

TO COOK IS TO LOVE

"No sooner met but they looked; no sooner looked

but they loved; no sooner loved but they sighed; no

sooner sighed but they . . ."

—William Shakespeare, <u>As You Like It</u>

The Long-term Culinary Meaning of Love

So it finally happened to *you*, eh? After all these days and nights, months and years, maybe even decades of searching for "the one," she is here and this is now. Savor the moment, my friend. Savor it here, and savor it now.

But most importantly, savor it on all those special occasions that mark your essential twoness.

Do not forget this. *Ever.*

Do not become one of those stupid, forgetful, forever haunted men who reneges on the first unwritten commandment of the relational ritual: Thou shalt not forget her birthday, or your anniversary. Or subparagraph A of the aforementioned clause: Thou shalt make that day *very* special. Or subparagraph B: Thou shalt honor this day with a special dinner.

Now I know a lot of you out there believe that "special dinner" refers to an evening out on the town, maybe dropping some big bucks in a fancy place for a Big Deal Dinner, eating unusual food that is exquisitely prepared by a Master Chef and served in an environment fit for a Queen. This will do nicely, but it is unnecessary. Unless you've been a *very* bad dog, in which case this astonishing show of guilt won't entirely redeem you, either.

In my experience, women appreciate the Big Deal Dinner because, at least in America, spending a lot of money is one way to show how much you care. Also because everyone does it. It is the relational equivalent of a cultural ritual at a time when most of our rituals are lost and most relational couples have forgotten the importance of inventing their own. That said, the larger issue for you to ponder here begins with this question: How should I demonstrate the personal meaning of our love to my beloved?

For a lot of men, this is a really difficult question, but it's not our fault. We live at a time in human history when the ready made, the quick and easy, the cliched, and the accessibility of a "guaranteed good time" in exchange for the imprint of a Visa card, all conspire to teach us to do unto each other what everyone else supposedly does. And to act like we enjoy it as much as they say they do. And to pay for it later.

This reduces the true meaning of relational rituals, which should be the genuine and creative celebration of our love, and our love world—what is intimately personal—to nothing more than another purchase decision. It reduces that which is sacred to that which is profane—another quick insertion of plastic into the good ol' ATM, another calculated drop in the overall balance that increasingly measures the worth of our lives.

This is not only regrettable, it is pitiful.

> No wonder there are so many troubled relationships! No wonder so many people view the mutual spending of money as the reason they stay together. And no wonder so many sad guys I know think that if they do this one thing, once or twice a year, they have satisfied the deep needs of their relational partners.

Unless the lady in question views the meaning of your relationship solely from the size of your wallet, these overt displays of plastic affluence are merely common and ordinary. There is nothing special about them because there is nothing personal in them. And if you *are* with a woman who values you for your money, then you are really in trouble. I wouldn't take out any big life insurance policies, either. She may be great in bed, have a fine body, provide witty insights into the work of Nietsche, and/or simply flatter the hell out of you, but she's not real. She is *dangerous*. She's teaching you that the only thing that matters is money, which is making you behave that way. She's sucking the soul from your body, man. Get out while you still can.

If diamonds are this girl's best friend, trust me, there is a reason for it. Think about that. Think about that real hard.

> Real women love personal expressions, not public displays. They value the small, thoughtful things that are done for them, *only*. The Big Deal Dinner may be nice, but it is far less compelling, certainly less meaningful, and less likely to be held in memory and recalled fondly than a thoughtful dinner prepared especially for her, by *you*, at home.

And no, I didn't say that just because I am the author of a cookbook.

I say it because it is true. In these postmodern times, this is one of the few truths you can dare call eternal.

It would be highly ironic if, after having said all that about the need to make these occasions special by preparing the meal she loves, I then provided you with the details of that meal. If I was able to do that, *you* should be suspicious. After all, how well do *I* know *your* woman? What I am advising you to do, therefore, is to figure out what she really likes, and make it for her.

Pretty simple, huh?

Bon appetit!

Giving Gifts

I have a friend, let's call him Mike, who regularly travels on business. At home is his lovely and loving wife, let's call her Carol, tending their children. Sometimes Mike is gone for weeks at a time.

One afternoon a group of us were hanging out together and the talk turned to travel. Mike had just returned from one of his long business trips. He regaled all of us at the table with tales of the deals on clothing, jewelry, and electronic items that could be had given the then-current state of the many overseas economies. He explained how he had loaded up a spare suitcase with new suits for himself, designer stuff that he got for a song.

We were "suitably" impressed.

"Ask him what he brought back for me," Carol said, her face deadpan and her eyes burning.

So I did.

"Nothing," Carol replied, before Mike could.

We were all more than a bit stunned. Mike said, in defense of himself, "Look, I don't know how to buy clothes for women, all right?" He looked around the table for moral support from the other guys. None was forthcoming.

Eventually someone changed changed the subject.

Mike is not an uncaring or particularly selfish husband. Nor is he a total jerk. What he believes about his lack of knowledge concerning women's clothing is what justifies, in his mind, his lack of gift giving. I hate to admit it, but I've known lots of guys like Mike. But even if there was a majority of men who believed and behaved like this, it still doesn't make it right.

A gift is something a man gives a woman because he wants to communicate his material appreciation for who she is, for what she does, for all that she means to him. But women interpret gifts a little bit differently. To them, *a gift is a sign of how you feel about your relationship*. By not being willing to learn what trinkets or baubles she likes, or to memorize her dress or sweater or lingerie size, or even simply to ask her about these things, what you are communicating to her *about your relationship* is what the French philosopher Jacques Derrida calls "the presence of an absence." Put simply, what she is hearing in the yawning absence of a gift is that something is equally absent from your heart.

And that is what hurts. It's not so much the price of the item, it is the fact that you remembered her. That you went just a little bit out of your way for her, that you were thinking about her. You need to do that. You need to do that *regularly*.

The price of an appropriate gift often troubles men. They complain that they don't know how much they should spend. In many cases this means they end up spending way too much, and the gift becomes—whether it is intended to or not—a message about guilt, or excess, or false hope, or just plain stupidity. In other cases they spend too little and it is received that way.

> The problem here is with an incorrect focus on the amount of money spent. It isn't really about money, guys. It is about the *symbolic value* of the gift within the overall story of the relationship. Think of a gift as an interpersonal emblem of what makes the two of you tick. Think of it as something material that contributes to your ongoing relational dialogue. Think of it as something that *only you* can truly provide *to and for her.*

To Cook is to Love

One guy I know kept a scrapbook of everything he and his girlfriend did together. He saved ticket stubs, photos, little stones from riverbeds, matches from restaurants, whatever. On Valentine's Day he presented her with the scrapbook, which, in addition to these items, contained poetry he had composed for her, and little stories of the times they had shared during that year. What this gift suggested was that he valued and remembered the times they spent together; its value far outweighed its cost. Another friend of mine, a metal sculptor and the designer of the cover of this book, makes his own Valentine's and birthday "cards" out of twisted pieces of metal, or bronzed, fabricated metal hearts. They are symbols that combine who he is with what she means to him, and each sculpture is a work that represents their relationship *for and about them*. The point here is that you need to devote a little skull time to these projects. Use your imagination. Make something whose meaning says: The strength of our love doesn't have a thing to do with money.

There is something else, another problem that must be dealt with. Some guys I have known think that if they give a special gift to a woman, this automatically means that the woman is supposed to give him something he wants in return. Probably you can flesh out the implications of this metaphor. This assumption, too, makes for a big relational mistake. It is to use the idea of a gift, as Marcel Mauss teaches us, as a kind of weapon, or as a tactical prison. It is to suggest that you are only giving it because you do, in fact, expect something of value in return.

Gifts given in the spirit of getting are despicable. They destroy the idea of gift-giving by cheapening what it should—and for many of us, *does*—stand for.

Gifts are symbols of love, they serve as personal signs of relational value.

Given in the proper spirit, for no reason other than a desire to please the one you love, they communicate a richness and depth of sentiment. They become the stuff of memories. They become part of the continuing, evolving story of "us."

Learn what they are, from your woman's perspective, and joyfully live within what you find there.

Give a gift that truly means something special. To both of you.

A NOTE ON WINE

Let's assume for a moment that you like to drink wine

with your meal. Let's also assume that she does.

Now let's reveal a terrible truth that lurks in the hearts

of some men: You really don't know very much at all

about choosing wine. Or about coordinating wines

with particular dinners.

Good, Reasonably-Priced Wines You Can Buy In Any Supermarket

Probably you drink the same stuff over and over again. "Because you like it," right? Maybe so, but it may also be because you don't know what else to buy.

It is true that you should drink what you enjoy, regardless of what the tonier advice columns say. After all, it's your money and it's what you like. Besides, choosing the right wine can be a daunting challenge. There are so many varieties, so many labels, so many vintages, from so many wine producing states, provinces, and countries, well, you understand. Unless you have a good local wine shop with a knowledgeable owner, or a good friend who really knows wines, chances are good that you buy your wine in the local supermarket by looking for the little "Wine Spectator" or other ratings cards used these days. Anything over 85 can't be *that* bad, right?

More or less. However, be sure that the vintage in the recommendation matches the vintage of the bottle on your grocer's shelf. In many cases, they don't. The difference between an '89 California Chardonnay (one of the best years, ever) and a '97 is vast. That doesn't mean that '97s are bad; it just means there will be a marked difference in the complexity of flavors that meet your taste buds. If you enjoy wine, it pays to acquire at least a modest understanding of vintages, and of wineries.

A Note on Wines

Rather than confront this level of complexity in a supermarket, some guys I know just grab a big ol' bottle of jug wine, figuring, as they put it "it's wine, ain't it?" Unfortunately, with this attitude there is no real opportunity to learn the quality differences between a $7 jug and a $12 one. And these are differences that matter, both to your palate and to the success of your meal.

Finally, some guys I have known *only* drink white wine. Why? Because they claim that red wines have given them serious hangovers, even when moderate amounts were consumed. Hence, by guy-logic, all red wines must be bad. The truth is that red wines are allowed more impurities, and some people have a bodily reaction to those impurities. But not *all* red wines are suspect. Why fail to appreciate the richness of a quality red wine just because you made a poor choice years ago?

This section can serve the average man's wine purchasing and coordinating needs. If you are a true connoisseur you can skip my recs and remain smug in your superiority. Fine by me. This chart is designed For The Rest of Us.

Sandwiches

Sandwiches generally go well with beer; if wine is chosen, the selection should complement the meat/cheese combination used. For turkey, pork, or chicken sandwiches, use a light white wine with more acidity, such as a Sauvignon Blanc or even a smoother Chablis or Zinfadel. If the meat is smoked, it can handle a firmer, toastier, oakiness, such as found in the classic California Chardonnays. For beef dishes, any good quality Burgundy or Cabernet is always welcome, and milder dishes generally do well accompanied by a fruity Beaujolais or blush Zinfadel. Or, any of the wines listed below:

> Columbia-Crest Sauvignon Blanc
> Chateau St. Michelle Sauvignon Blanc
> Beringer White Zinfadel
> Glen Ellen White Zinfadel

Rodney Strong Chardonnay

Dry Creek Chardonnay

Indigo Hills Chardonnay

Tessera Cabernet Sauvignon

Meridian Cabernet Sauvignon

Beaujolais-Villages (any label)

Beringer Gamay Beaujolais

Gallo White Grenache

Salads

Any good quality white or blush wine. I recommend:

Kendall-Jackson Sauvignon Blanc

Duckhorn Sauvignon Blanc

Chalk Hill Sauvignon Blanc

Blossom Hill White Zinfadel

Westbend Chardonnay

Hess Select Chardonnay

Napa Ridge Gewurtraminer

Trefethen Dry Reisling

Chateau St. Michelle Reisling

Pasta, with Red Sauces

The darker and spicier the sauce, the richer the red wine ought to be. I recommend:

> Chianti Classico
>
> Bolla Bordolino
>
> Louis Jadot Beaujolais
>
> Stone Creek Zinfadel
>
> Kenwood Zinfadel
>
> Forest Glen Sangiovese
>
> La Crema Pinot Noir
>
> Estancia Pinot Noir
>
> Chateau Souvrain Merlot
>
> Bogle Merlot
>
> Forest Glenn Cabernet Sauvignon
>
> Beautour Cabernet Sauvignon
>
> Rodney Strong Cabernet Sauvignon
>
> Firestone Cabernet Sauvignon

Pasta, with White Sauces, No Sauce, or Veggies

The lighter and milder the sauce, the lighter the white wine or blush Zinfadel ought to be.

> Sutter Home White Zinfadel
>
> Fetzer White Zinfadel
>
> Silverado Sauvignon Blanc
>
> William Hill Sauvignon Blanc
>
> Columbia-Crest Reisling
>
> Alderbrook Gewurtraminer
>
> Beringer Appelation Collection Chardonnay
>
> Barton & Guestier (B&G)Saint-Louis Chardonnay

Tex-Mex

Hot chilis numb the taste buds and tongue. In most cases, you want a dry white wine with a lot of fruitiness: Sauvignon Blanc; Pinot Blanc; or Australian or Chilean Chardonnays. Red wines should be selected for low acidity and rich fruit flavor, as in red Zinfadels, Syrahs, Merlots, or California Gamay Beaujolais and Pinot Noirs. For grilled foods, you need a hearty burgundy, such as a Cabernet Sauvignon.

> Clos du Bois Sauvignon Blanc
> Groth Sauvignon Blanc
> Chateau St. Michelle Sauvignon Blanc
> Santa Rita "120" Chardonnay
> Concha y Toro Marques Chardonnay
> Mirassou Merlot
> Silver Ridge Merlot
> Robert Mondavi Zinfadel
> Beautoir Zinfadel
> Buena Vista Pinot Noir
> Wild Horse Pinot Noir
> Monterra Petit Sirah
> Bogle Petit Sirah

A Note on Wines

Thai, Japanese, Korean

Assertive and distinctive spicing such as that provided by cumin, coriander, ginger, garlic, lemon grass, anise, and curry powder call for a spicy wine that can hold up against these challenges. Gewurztraminers, Vouvray, and Reislings are moderately sweet and spicy, and make good choices among white wines, a fruity Beaujolais, Zinfadel, or soft Merlot will suit those whose palate tends to favor the reds.

> Geyser Peak Gewurtraminer
> Barton & Guestier (B&G) Vouvray
> Chateau St. Michelle Reisling
> Beringer Reisling
> Beringer Gamay Beaujolais
> Jadot Beaujolais
> Dry Creek Merlot
> Silver Ridge Merlot
> Chateau Souvrain Merlot
> Kenwood Zinfadel

Chicken

Chardonnay for roasts and barbecues or any chicken dish with a white cream sauce; Pinot Gris for spicy chicken salads; a Gewurztraminer or blush Zinfadel for stir-frys; and a Sauvignon Blanc or Pinot Blanc for sandwiches.

> Clos du Bois Chardonnay
> Hess Select Chardonnay
> Clos du Val Chardonnay
> Ecco Domani Pinot Grigio
> Fontana Candida Pinot Grigio
> Beringer Gewurtraminer
> Napa Ridge Gewurtraminer
> Fetzer White Zinfadel

Sutter Home Zinfadel

Beringer Zinfadel

Columbia-Crest Sauvignon Blanc

Geyser Peak Sauvignon Blanc

Cow

Cabernet Sauvignon or Merlot for any red meat that is grilled or roasted. Stews and chilies can stand a Shiraz or sturdy red Zinfadel. Black Opal Cabernet Merlot is an interesting blend of two recommended grapes.

Cavit Merlot

Georges Duboeuf Cabernet Sauvignon.

Robert Mondavi Cabernet, Opus One.

Forest Glen Cabernet Sauvignon

Santa Rita Reserva Cabernet

Casa Lapostolle Cabernet

Pig

Same as chicken.

Seafood

Chardonnay for richer grilled fillets or baked dishes, or anything served with a cream sauce. Sauvignon Blanc for shellfish or seafood salads.

Rosemont Estate Chardonnay

Cavit Pinot Grigio Delle Venizie

See list for Salads for Sauvignon Blanc and additional Chardonnay recommendations

Breakfast in Bed

Champaigne, only. I prefer Brut or Extra Dry. The higher quality, the better . . .

INDEX

Index

W